BRIGHTON CHURCHES

BY THE SAME AUTHOR

Fashionable Brighton 1820–1860
The History and Architecture of Brighton
About Brighton
Brighton Old and New
James Wyatt
Brighton Town and Brighton People
The Theatre Royal, Brighton
The Wagners of Brighton (jointly with Sir Anthony Wagner)

BRIGHTON CHURCHES

Antony Dale

R

ROUTLEDGE

First published in 1989
by Routledge
11 New Fetter Lane, London EC4P 4EE

Filmset in Bembo
and printed in Great Britain by
BAS Printers Limited, Over Wallop, Hampshire

British Library CIP Data

Dale, Antony, 1912–
Brighton churches.
1. East Sussex. Brighton Churches: history
I. Title
942.2'56

ISBN 0-415-00863-8

CONTENTS

CONTENTS

ILLUSTRATIONS

ACKNOWLEDGEMENTS

Plates nos. 4, 5, 6, 9, 11, 12, 17, 18, 19, 22, 25, 30, 32, 33, 49, 50, 51, 52, 53, 58, 60, and 63 are reproduced by kind permission of the Director of the Brighton Museum & Art Gallery.

Plates 13, 20, 21, 23, 38, 39, 44, 47, and 62 are reproduced by kind permission of the Royal Commission on the Historical Monuments of England.

Plate 14 is reproduced by kind permission of Mr J. S. Gray.

Plate 29 is reproduced by kind permission of Sir Anthony Wagner.

The other photographs were taken by J. W. R. Barrow.

INTRODUCTION

Brighton is famous for many things, but chiefly for its Regency architecture. Most of this was built during the ten years of George IV's reign as King, rather than in the actual Regency. The number of houses in the town doubled during that decade. To provide for their ecclesiastical needs eight chapels of ease were built during the first thirty years of the nineteenth century. The architectural and social history of the town naturally did not stop with the accession of William IV. Indeed, both received a considerable fillip from the arrival of the railway from London in 1841. This boost really lasted for the rest of the century and was reflected in the quantity and quality of the churches which were erected. Of these, at least six are outstanding and can stand comparison with the nineteenth-century churches of any other town. They are in fact the second architectural accomplishment that Brighton has to show.

Almost equally remarkable were the clergy who built them and ministered there. Our age tends to look back on the Victorian period as an age of clerical impoverishment. No doubt many of its clergymen, particularly curates, were in fact very poor. But not in Brighton. Because of its fashionable nature, this town attracted a large number of well-to-do but devoted men who were rich enough to build their own chapels of ease or churches at their own expense; or, if these had already been built, to buy them from the preceding clergymen, and then to provide there the particular degree of churchmanship which they favoured, whether this was ritualist, as the High Church move-ment was then called, or Evangelical. Amongst these men were the Wagners, father and son, who dominated the ecclesiastical life of Brighton for about fifty years from 1824 onwards, the brothers Anderson, the brothers Elliott, James O'Brien, Frederick Reade and F. W. Robertson. Robertson of

Brighton alone amongst that number was not rich. This book, therefore, is concerned not only with the architectural quality of Brighton's churches but also with the story of how they came to be built and were at first administered.

From about 1880 onwards both Brighton and Hove grew so large that new churches became very numerous. At the same time their architectural quality declined. So broadly speaking this book does not cover churches that were built after 1880. Two exceptions, both by J. L. Pearson, (St Barnabas's and All Saints, Hove), were too good to be omitted.

Strangely enough, not much printed attention has been given to these nineteenth-century Brighton churches. From 1881 to 1883 John Sawyer wrote a series of articles in the *Sussex Daily News* which were published together soon afterwards under the title of *Brighton Churches*. This is now a very rare book. It deals not only with the churches of the Church of England but with those of other Christian denominations and also the synagogue in Middle Street. The present book follows Sawyer in not being confined solely to Anglican churches.

The only other general source is the brilliant series of articles by H. S. Goodhart-Rendel in the *Architectural Review* of 1918. But in the short space of three articles he could necessarily deal with each building only very briefly and mention only its principal architectural features. Also, since the articles are now nearly seventy years old they need bringing up to date in some respects, although surprisingly few of the opinions expressed by Goodhart-Rendel have not stood the test of time. He undoubtedly knew more about Brighton churches than anyone else either before or since.

Since 1880 and 1918 both Brighton and Hove have expanded considerably. These expansions have brought within their boundaries a number of previously separate villages or settlements. These all had medieval parish churches of their own which are of considerable distinction. These churches have been included in the present book to complete the picture of Brighton churches today.

ST NICHOLAS'S CHURCH
(the old parish church)

In 1086 the Domesday survey declared that there was a church in Brighthelmston, as Brighton was first called. A few years later the church was granted by the lord of the manor to the great Cluniac priory of St Pancras at Southover, Lewes, which retained it until the Reformation. It is not certain where this original church stood. The earliest Brighthelmston was below the cliff. It is possible, though unlikely, that the first church stood there. But it is generally assumed that it was built on the existing site of St Nicholas. Some evidence to this effect is provided by the fact that some stones of Norman date were incorporated in the fourteenth-century tower when this was built. The only other surviving Norman work is the font, which is the chief glory of the church. The settlement below the cliff was gradually eroded by the sea, and a newer town on a simple grid-iron pattern was built within the boundaries of the present East, North and West Streets. If a new site was chosen for the church at this time it was selected with the triple object of providing a landmark for seafarers, safe-guarding the building from further sea erosion and protecting it from attacks by the French, who, throughout the Middle Ages, landed all along the Sussex coast and burned the settlements which they found. That this was not a vain precaution was shown in 1514, when Brighton's turn came. The French landed there and burned virtually the whole town, from which only St Nicholas's church on its hill escaped.

The surviving medieval building dates from the mid-fourteenth century and comprised originally a chancel, a nave with aisles and a west tower. In the fifteenth century a chantry chapel was added to the south of the chancel. This projected beyond the width of the south aisle. In 1537 the last prior of Southover priory surrendered the living to the Crown, which granted

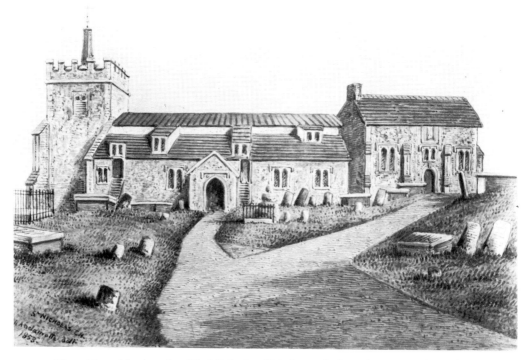

1 The old parish church of St Nicholas, Brighton, before the restoration of 1853. Drawing by W. A. Delamotte

it in 1540 to Thomas Cromwell, in 1541 to Queen Anne of Cleves and in 1558 to the Bishop of Chichester. The Bishop of Chichester has remained the patron of the living ever since.

In the eighteenth century the church was fitted with box-pews, which were arranged in the pattern of a cross with the font at the central point. As Brighton began to expand from 1750 onwards and as there was no other Anglican place of worship in the town, the church became inadequate to the needs of the congregation. Galleries were therefore built on every side, including the east end over the chancel arch and with its back to the altar. These galleries were entered from outside staircases. From that date until 1853 the church bore a strong resemblance to Whitby church in Yorkshire, which still has multiple galleries approached from outside staircases. The reredos under the east window was a triptych of panels containing the Ten Commandments, flanked by pilasters with a pediment over.

In the early years of the nineteenth century the position grew worse, despite the fact that several new chapels of ease were built in the town in the 1820s. St Nicholas's was the only church where the sittings were free. Several hun-

2

2 The interior of St Nicholas's church before the restoration of 1853

dred people were turned away every Sunday. The church was also in very bad condition. It was at that time the law of the land that the Vestry (that is, the inhabitants who were assessed to the parish poor-rate) were liable for the upkeep of the parish church and the maintenance of divine services there. But Brighton contained a large number of Non-conformists, to whom this seemed a most unjust provision. The vicar of the time, the Rev. Henry Michell Wagner, was a high Tory, but most of his parishioners were Radicals. From 1835 onwards a running battle developed between the vicar and the Vestry meetings, at which funds for the repair of the church were often refused. The state of the church became so serious that some of the windows in the chancel were boarded up. From this deadlock the church was rescued by the death of the Duke of Wellington on 14 September 1852.

As a boy the Duke had been a pupil at the academy for young gentlemen which was established at the old vicarage in Nile Street in Brighton by H. M. Wagner's grandfather and predecessor as vicar, the Rev. Henry Michell. The

Duke had therefore worshipped at St Nicholas's church at that time. Wagner had also been tutor to the Duke's two sons from 1818 to 1826. Within a week of the Duke's death Wagner called a public meeting at the Town Hall in Brighton, at which it was decided to restore the parish church as a memorial to the Duke. The vicar headed the subscription list with the gift of £1,000. The sum of £4,948. 16s. was swiftly raised, which had been consistently refused as part of a compulsory church rate.

The ecclesiastical faculty which was issued on 15 April 1853 actually authorised the demolition and rebuilding of the old church, and it was typical of the lack of respect shown to medieval buildings, particularly those containing Georgian fittings that T. W. Horsfield in his *History of Sussex*, which was published in 1835, described St Nicholas's church as 'a tasteless and unsightly edifice . . . in all respects below mediocrity.' The work of restoration was entrusted to Richard Cromwell Carpenter. The contractors were Messrs Bushby of Littlehampton. The work was completed in the extremely short period of nine months. R. C. Carpenter was an architect much favoured by the Tractarians in those early days of the Gothic revival for his treatment of Gothic churches. But, like so many Victorian architects, he lacked the feeling that medieval work was better than anything which he could do in his own time. His restoration of St Nicholas's was therefore very little short of a complete rebuilding. The whole church was re-roofed. In order to provide extra accommodation Carpenter demolished the outer walls of the fourteenth-century aisles and rebuilt them to more than double their original width, except for the fifteenth-century south chapel, which he reduced in width. The new north aisle was extended at the west end so as to be level with the west wall of the tower, and at the east end to form an organ-chamber and vestry north of the chancel. Between the chancel and the south chapel the twin-arcade was replaced by a single arch. The tower arch was unblocked. A new east window was inserted. All the galleries and box-pews were taken down as they were an anathema to the Tractarians. The font was removed to its present position to the west of the south doorway. All the monuments were banished to the west end of the church. The screen was spared but repainted. The old organ had been in the west gallery, and so was temporarily removed for safe-keeping to the Royal Pavilion. But when the time came to insert it in the new organ-chamber to the north of the chancel it proved too large to go in. So the church was without a proper organ for nearly twenty years.

These alterations, although they did increase the amount of seating on the ground, actually reduced the total accommodation available in the church from 1,300 to 900 owing to the abolition of the galleries. Carpenter added one new feature of considerable distinction. This was a specific memorial to the Duke of Wellington in the form of a miniature Eleanor cross in stone, which is now at the west end of the north aisle.

The total cost of the rebuilding was £5,769. The church was reopened for worship on 8 April 1854. Carpenter died in the next year and was himself commemorated in the church. In the step which separated the original south aisle from the south chapel a small brass plate was inserted which read: 'In memory of R. C. Carpenter who but a short time survived the completion of his design, the restoration of the church MDCCCLV.' It seems not to be recorded when this brass plate was removed, but that it has disappeared is perhaps symbolic of the even greater lack of respect shown by a later age to Carpenter's work than he had shown to the medieval building. Both are regrettable.

Carpenter had removed the three-decker pulpit of the old church and substituted a wooden one of one tier. In 1867 this was replaced by an open-work iron pulpit. This was the gift of Somers Clarke, who was Vestry clerk from 1830 to 1892 and a close friend of the vicar, the Rev. H. M. Wagner. It was designed by his architect son, Somers Clarke junior, who was later to do other work to the church. The 1870s saw considerable new work at the church. A new organ was inserted in 1872, which cost £500. In 1876-7 a choir vestry was added to the north-west of the organ-chamber. This was also designed by Somers Clarke junior and cost £842. Two years later he provided new stalls and panelling for the chancel. The panels of the reredos were painted by Mathew Ridley Corbet. To enable the work to be effected Somers Clarke senior purchased and redeemed the rectorial tithes. The cost of the work was borne by Henry Waldron Smithers, whose family owned a brewery at old Portslade. He was a churchwarden of the church and mayor of Brighton in 1861-2. He died in 1884 and a memorial to him was erected towards the west end of the north aisle.

Most of the stained glass dates from this period (1878-87). This was designed by Charles Eamer Kemp, who always called himself Kempe. He was a Brighton man, first cousin of Thomas Read Kemp, the founder of Kemp Town, and son of Nathaniel Kemp of Preston manor and later of Ovingdean Hall. In 1824 Nathaniel Kemp had given to the church two silver chalices, two patens and a flagon. One of the windows in the south wall of the chancel also was the gift of Somers Clarke senior in memory of his old friend, H. M. Wagner, who had died in 1870.

In 1882 the east window, which had been designed by R. C. Carpenter and inserted in 1853, was given to the new church of the Annunciation in Washington Street, Brighton, and the existing Perpendicular window was erected in its place.

The next work dates from 1892. The church was evidently very dark, so the whole roof was raised by mechanical means and clerestory windows inserted. The supervision of this work was again entrusted to Somers Clarke junior. This fact is recorded on one of the roof-beams, although the inscription cannot be seen from the ground. The roof was also painted by Charles Eamer Kempe.

The enlarged spaces over the chancel and tower arches which were the result of raising the roof, were then filled with mural paintings. These were designed by Somers Clarke and painted by Charles Eamer Kempe. The western wall shows the Royal arms, copied from a hatchment and flanked by angels with, above, the arms of William de Warenne who founded Southover priory, and the arms of the diocese of Chichester. The murals on the east wall are most unusual. They represent a flower design inspired by a William Morris wallpaper, but the flowers themselves are of embossed metal incorporated in the painting. The paintings are perhaps unique in this respect. Both murals were restored in 1972 by the Regency Society of Brighton and Hove on the advice of Dr Kenneth Hempel of the Victoria and Albert Museum.

In 1900 the south chapel was slightly enlarged. The cost was borne by a legacy under the will of Mary Viscountess Combermere, who had died as far back as 1889. She was the daughter of Robert and Barbara Gibbings, who are commemorated by a tablet in the south-east corner of the chapel. At the same time the Wellington memorial, which had stood in this chapel since 1853, was removed to the west end of the north aisle. In 1909 the chapel was converted into a Lady chapel. But the figure of the Virgin over the altar, which dates from the fifteenth century, was added by the congregation in memory of Canon Charles Watson Bond, who was vicar of the church from 1887 to 1910. The statue of St Nicholas outside the chapel was erected in memory of Bishop Hugh Maudsley Hordern, who was vicar from 1910 to 1924 and subsequently Bishop of Lewes. It was designed by Sir Ninian

3 St Nicholas's church 1987

Comper. The gates adjoining it were added after the Second World War as a memorial to the men of the Royal Sussex Regiment who fell at Dunkirk.

The result of all this nineteenth-century and later restoration and rebuilding is that the church has very little medieval work to show. Of the exterior there is only the fourteenth-century tower, and of the interior, only the arcades of the nave and the chancel arch. The most important internal fitting is the splendid circular twelfth-century font. This is of course older than the surviving medieval part of the church and must have come either from the older building on the site or from an older church below the cliff, or from Southover priory, Lewes, which owned the Brighton living before the Reformation. The font is of Caen stone and Byzantine in feeling. Round the bowl are carved four scenes. The first is of the Baptism of Christ. The central figure is shown partly immersed in water and flanked by the figures of St John the Baptist and an angel. The next scene is of the Last Supper, showing Christ with six disciples. The two smaller panels represent scenes

7

from the life of St Nicholas: the innkeeper of Myra confessing to the murder of three youths, and the rescue of pilgrims who had accepted from the devil, disguised as a woman, a vessel of oil which St Nicholas bids them cast into the sea. The carved oak font-cover dates from 1857. In 1745 the church-wardens of the time, H. Stanbridge and W. Burcholl, had their names inscribed on the base of the font. The inscription was removed in the mid-nineteenth-century restoration of the church. J. A. Erredge in his *History of Brighton*, published in 1862, says that the inscription of these churchwardens' names was a 'monument to their vitiated taste, confirmed vanity and profound ignorance.'

The only other medieval fixture which survived the restoration of 1853 was the rood-screen between the nave and the chancel. This probably dates from the late fourteenth century and is of a pattern which is common in Norfolk but rare in Sussex. It is of eight bays, of which the two centre bays occupy the position of a doorway. The lower portion is solid with two panels to each bay, which were painted with figures. In the eighteenth century the whole screen was painted white. In 1853 the white paint was removed and the screen repainted. It was also found that the western part of the upper portion had been cut away. This could have been to make room for the old east gallery, or perhaps the screen was brought from elsewhere and re-versed. In 1887 the screen was again restored. The original projection was replaced, but no trace of a medieval rood-loft was discovered. This work was executed at the expense of John Leonard Brigden in memory of his wife, Mary, who had died the year before. He had been mayor of Brighton from 1863 to 1865. When he died in 1903 a memorial to him was erected at the east end of the north aisle. The figures surmounting the rood-screen were not added until 1917.

Bell-ringing was always a feature of St Nicholas's church. In 1777 a peal of ten bells was cast for the church by Thomas Rudhall of Gloucester. Metal from earlier bells was probably used in the casting. Two of these bells were given to St Peter's church, Brighton, in 1828 when it became a chapel of ease to the parish church. They were replaced in 1892 as the result of a legacy from George Shelley who had been a churchwarden for ten years. The whole peal was recast in 1922. When Brighton became fashionable the bells were frequently rung to mark the arrival in the town of important persons, particularly the Sovereign. On one occasion William IV arrived on a Sunday. The bells were silent and the King inquired why. He was told by the vicar, the

Rev. H. M. Wagner, that on Sunday the bells were only rung for the King of Kings. Queen Adelaide is said to have approved of this reply. The walls of the ringing chamber in the base of the tower are lined with tablets recording special marathon peals rung between 1777 and 1887, the last occasion being Queen Victoria's golden jubilee. These peals are also recorded in a bound volume by George F. Attree. The tablets in the tower were cleaned a few years ago by the Regency Society of Brighton and Hove.

The memorials in the body of the church are perhaps less unusual and have not fared well as most of them were banished by R. C. Carpenter to the west end of the nave, where they cannot be seen clearly. The most remarkable of these is that commemorating the great Duke of Wellington. This was designed by R. C. Carpenter in 1853 and carved by a sculptor named Phillip of Vauxhall. It takes the form of a miniature Eleanor cross, surmounted by a statue of St George. Within the cross is a central shaft of darker stone, round which winds a scroll inscribed with the names of Wellington's victories. Halfway up the cross a brass inscription records that the church was restored in the Duke's name. This cross originally stood at the east end of the south chapel, but in 1900 it was banished to a dark corner at the west end of the north aisle. The wheel has gone full circle, and the cross is recognised as being a fine work of art in its own right. It should really be moved to a more prominent part of the church where it could be seen to better advantage, but this would be very costly. It has, however, been recently cleaned and restored by the Regency Society of Brighton and Hove, and a spot-light has been installed so that it can be seen more clearly in its present position.

Of the memorials fixed to the walls only three are of any artistic pretension. In the dark south-east corner of the Lady chapel is a tablet showing two sorrowing female figures. This was erected in 1844 in memory of Robert Gibbings and his wife, Barbara. It was placed there by their daughter, Mary Viscountess Combermere. Under the terms of the latter's will the whole chapel was later restored and enlarged. The second interesting tablet is on the north wall of the north aisle. It commemorates Frances Corbie, the wife of Charles Corfield, who died in 1830. It shows an angel conducting her soul to heaven. Thirdly, on the west wall of the south aisle is a bust by Sir Richard Westmacott (1775–1856) of his wife Dorothy Margaret, daughter of Dr Wilkinson of Jamaica, who died on a visit to Brighton in 1834. In a similar position in the north aisle is a tablet to Susan Mansfield, wife of

Sir James Mansfield, Lord Chief Justice of the Common Pleas, who died in 1818. She and her husband lived at Marlborough House in Old Steine. Adjoining this memorial is a tablet to Thomas Read Kemp, who was one of the lords of the manor of Brighton and the founder of Kemp Town. His family vault and that of the Friend family, prosperous mercers of Lewes from whom the Kemps derived much of their property, is below the chancel. Thomas Read Kemp actually died in Paris in 1844 and was buried there in Père la Chaise cemetery.

Another burial in a vault below the church and of which there is no visible memorial was of an infant son named Ralph of Hester and Henry Thrale, the friends of Dr Johnson. The child died in 1775 when his parents were staying at their Brighton house in West Street. Only one post from the post-and-chain fence in front of this house survives today. Dr Johnson frequently stayed with the Thrales there, although he did not like Brighton. In 1909, the bicentenary of Johnson's birth, his attendance at St Nicholas's church was commemorated by the erection of a small brass plate in the splay of the easternmost window in the north aisle. This is said to have been placed near to the position where the Thrales had their pew in the unrestored church.

Three mayors of Brighton who had extensive connections with the church are commemorated. Henry Smithers and John Brigden have already been mentioned as benefactors to the church. The third was Henry Martin, who was mayor in 1865–6 and who also wrote a book on Brighton, *The History of Brighton and Environs from the Earliest Period to the Present Day*. His tablet is to the north of the tower arch. He died in 1906.

More interesting than the tablets in the church are the memorials in the church-yard. This burial-ground was landscaped by Brighton Council soon after the Second World War, but all the historic tombs were left in their original positions. The oldest and probably the most interesting of these is that of Captain Nicholas Tattersell, who took Charles II to France in 1651. This is a table-tomb adjoining the south wall of the church to the east of the porch. After the Battle of Worcester the King made his way south to Dorset and Hampshire, accompanied by Lord Wilmot and Colonel Gunter. After a preliminary reconnaissance they found in the then remote creek of Shoreham a coal brig named the *Surprise* of which Tattersell was the captain. They offered Tattersell £80 for a passage to France. Tattersell, who almost certainly knew what he was being asked to do, demanded £200 and also their bond. The bond was refused since the word of a gentleman should suffice, but the increased sum was agreed. It was a purely financial transaction. The King landed safely in Normandy on 15 October 1651.

When Charles II returned in 1660 naturally it was alleged that the motives involved had been wholly those of royalism. Tattersell's claims were too good to be denied. He was given a hereditary pension of £100 a year. His ship was taken into the Royal Navy as a fifth-rate ship of the line and renamed *The Royal Escape*. The ship was painted by Van der Velde, and the picture is in the Royal collection in Buckingham Palace. Tattersell became a great man in Brighton – High Constable and a great persecutor of Dissenters. He died in 1674. The inscription on his tomb is as follows:

> Within this marble monument doth lie
> Approved faith, honour and loyalty;
> In this cold clay he has now ta'en up his station
> Who once preserved the Church, the Crowne and Nation.
> When Charles the Greate was nothing but a breath
> This ualient soul stept tweene him and Death
> Usurpers' threats nor tyrant rebels' frowne
> Could not affright his duty to the crowne;
> Which glorious act of his, for church and state
> Eight princes in one day did gratulate –
> Professing all to him in debt to bee,
> As all the world are to his memory.
> Since Earth could not reward the worth him given
> He now receives it from the King of Heaven.
> In the same chest one jewel more you have,
> The partner of his virtues, bed and grave.

One has the impression that these virtues, save perhaps the last two lines, were largely imaginary and that Captain Tattersell was a rather unpleasant person.

Just across the path to the south-east from Captain Tattersell's tomb is the grave of a more local celebrity, Phoebe Hessell, the woman soldier. She was born at Stepney in 1713 and at the age of 15 fell in love with a soldier named William Golding. When his regiment was ordered overseas she concealed her sex and enlisted as a man in another regiment which was also bound for the West Indies. She served for seventeen years without her sex being discovered and was even wounded in the arm at the battle of Fontenoy in 1745. It was not until her lover was himself wounded and invalided home that she revealed her sex to the wife of her commanding officer and obtained her discharge. She and Golding were then married and lived happily together for twenty years. After his death she moved to Brighton and married again. Her second husband, William Hessell, died before 1797. By that time she was 84 and subsisted partly by selling gingerbread and apples in the street and partly through the receipt of poor-rate relief. In the last years of her life, possibly from 1806 onwards, she received a pension of ten shillings a week from the Prince of Wales, afterwards George IV, who had heard of her romantic story. She lived to see him become King, and in the local procession on the occasion of his coronation rode in the vicar of Brighton's carriage as the oldest local inhabitant. She died on 12 December 1821 aged 108, having been born in the reign of Queen Anne. Her tombstone was erected at the expense of Hyam Lewis, a local jeweller and pawnbroker, who was one of the first Jews to be a Town Commissioner. It was recently restored and relettered by the Northumberland Fusiliers, who are the successors to the Fifth Foot regiment in which she served, and who have always considered her to be a member of their regiment. A portrait of her hangs in their mess.

Just behind Phoebe Hessell's tomb and slightly to the north is the grave of a contemporary of hers: Martha Gunn, the bathing woman. When Dr Richard Russell first recommended people to bathe in the sea in 1750 very few people could swim. They therefore had to be bathed by dippers for men and bathers for women. A private bathing-machine was drawn by a horse into the water. The horse was then turned back with his face to the land. The dipper or bather stood on the steps of the machine and plunged the 'bathee' several times into the water. The most famous of these operators were 'Smoaker' Miles for men and Martha Gunn for women. The latter came of an old-established Brighton family of fishermen. Their connection with the sea is still maintained by a fish shop in St James's Street which has one of the oldest shop-fronts in Brighton. All the most prominent women who came to Brighton in the second half of the eighteenth century were bathed by Martha Gunn. She became a local celebrity who was a favourite of the Prince of Wales, afterwards George IV, and was a frequent visitor to the first or Holland's Royal Pavilion. In 1796 the Prince commissioned a portrait of her holding a child from the pastel artist, John Russell, RA. This was exhibited in the Royal Academy of that year. It is still in the Royal collection and hangs in Buckingham Palace. Martha Gunn lived to be 88 and died on 2 May 1815. 'Smoaker' Miles was also buried in St Nicholas's church-yard, in the north-west corner near the west boundary wall. But the inscription of the tombstone had already become indecipherable by 1862, when Erredge's *History of Brighton* was published, and no doubt the tombstone itself was one of those that was moved when the church-yard was landscaped after the Second World War.

To the north of Martha Gunn's tomb and backing onto the church-yard wall along Church Street is a memorial in the form of a Coadeware stone urn which is the most elegant tomb in the burial-ground. This is the grave of the singer and actress Anna Maria Crouch. She was born on 20 April 1763 and was the third of the six children of Peregrine Phillips and a French mother. He was a lawyer who gave public readings of poetry. Her first teacher in music was an organist named Wafer at the Berwick Street chapel. She was then articled for three years as a singing pupil to Thomas Linley. She made her first appearance at Drury Lane Theatre on 11 November 1783 in the role of Mandane in Arne's *Artaxerxes*. She was engaged at that theatre for six seasons at a salary of between £6 and £12 a night. This was the beginning of a life-long connection with Drury Lane. In addition to singing roles like Clarissa in *Lionel and Clarissa* she also took speaking parts in plays such as Garrick's *The Clandestine Marriage*, and even played Ophelia opposite John Kemble's Hamlet. In 1784, when playing in Ireland during the summer, she eloped with the son of a Roman Catholic Irish peer but was overtaken before they could be married. The next year she married Lieutenant Crouch of the Royal Navy. They had one son who lived only two days.

Much the most important association of her life was her attachment to the famous singer Michael Kelly. In 1787, after a career spent mostly at the Royal Opera House in Naples and the Imperial Opera House in Vienna, he became the resident composer and principal tenor at Drury Lane Theatre. It is said that Mrs Crouch had to reteach him English while he taught her Italian vocalisation. She fell in love with Kelly, and he joined the Crouch household in a 'ménage à trois'. But when she later had a passing association with the Prince of Wales, Lieutenant Crouch cut up rough and departed. She, however, agreed to pay her husband an allowance. This sort of arrangement seems to have been common form in associations between actresses and naval officers at the period. When her contemporary rival, Dorothy Jordan, was living with the Duke of Clarence, his debts were so great that the actress's salary must have been a welcome addition to their household expenses. Kelly and Mrs Crouch established themselves at a house in Pall Mall, where the Prince of Wales, Sheridan and Stephen Storace were frequent guests.

Mrs Crouch continued singing principal roles for nearly twenty years, but towards the end of her career concentrated more on training other singers. She retired from the stage for health reasons in 1801. A suggestion has been made that this condition was not unconnected with drink, but this may well have been a libel. She died at Brighton on 2 October 1805, possibly as the result of an internal injury due to a fall. Her tombstone was erected by Michael Kelly. Now that she is herself largely forgotten, the interest in her grave is perhaps due principally to the fact that the memorial was erected by a colleague of Mozart's and the original Don Basilio and Don Curzio in the first performance of *The Marriage of Figaro*.

Mrs Crouch's success as a singer and actress was probably as much due to her beauty as to her talents. Kelly himself said of her: 'she seemed to aggregate in herself all that was exquisite and charming.' Another critic wrote that 'her appearance was that of a meteor. It dazzled from excess of brilliancy every spectator.' She was painted by Romney, Lawrence and E. Harding. Romney's enchanting portrait of her can be seen in the Iveagh Collection at Kenwood House, Hampstead.

Across the pathway to the west of Anna Maria Crouch's tomb and in the enclosed part of the church-yard to the north of the church is the grave of a more local celebrity: Sake Deen Mahomed, who introduced Turkish baths, or 'shampooing' as it was then called, into England. He was born at Patna in India in 1749 and studied to be a surgeon under the East India Company. He later came to England and, after a brief visit to Ireland where he eloped with an Irish girl, established a vapour bath in Brighton in 1786. This stood on the site of the present Queen's Hotel facing west along the promenade. The establishment became in due course very successful. Mahomed claimed to have effected cures for such illnesses as asthma, paralysis, rheumatism, sciatica and lumbago. He decorated his baths with the discarded crutches and surgical implements of his cured patients, like a votive chapel in a Roman Catholic country. A French visitor to Brighton in 1827, the comte Auguste Louis Charles de la Garde, describes how the patient was enveloped in a flannel tent filled with perfumed steam, into which two arms belonging to an invisible body were thrust from outside to massage the patient. In Moscow and Constantinople the massage had been performed visibly by a scantily dressed girl serf or slave. But in England 'la pudeur anglaise' decreed otherwise.

Mahomed was in due course appointed 'shampooing surgeon to His Majesty King George IV' and frequently went to the Royal Pavilion to massage the King in the bath-room which George IV had installed in the King's apartments on the ground floor. This appointment was continued by King William IV. Mahomed's court dress for the office has been preserved in the Brighton Museum.

Mahomed wrote several books, including *Travels*, published in Cork in 1794, and *Shampooing, or benefits resulting from the use of the Indian vapour bath*. He lived to the age of 102 and died on 24 February 1851. There is also a portrait of him in the Brighton Museum. His son, Arthur Akhbar Mahomed, carried on his baths until the 1870s. The building was eventually pulled down to make way for the Queen's Hotel.

Towards the eastern end of the church-yard is the table-tomb of a local benefactor named Swan Downer. He was a Brighton man who made a fortune in trade in London. When he died in 1816 he left £5,000 to provide clothing for forty-eight poor men and women. The recipients were given two sets of clothing a year, but that of the women at least was very old-fashioned: mob caps, coal-scuttle bonnets, sleeve mittens, black woollen shawls and red flannel petticoats. Swan Downer also bequeathed £10,106. 15s. 3d. to endow a school for twenty poor girls. This was established in 1819 at 12 Gardner Street, Brighton. The building, which later became a public house named the Sussex Arms, formerly had an inscription on it recording the endowment. It is now a shop. In 1867 the school moved to 11 Dyke Road (formerly Church Hill). This interesting Gothic building was designed by George Somers Clarke junior. It later became a private house and is now a discotheque. The girls of the school also wore a distinctive uniform with white collars and cuffs. They sat in the west gallery of St Nicholas's church.

Further down the slope to the east is the tomb which has probably the most interesting design of any in the church-yard. This commemorates the architect, Amon Wilds who, with his partner, Charles Augustus Busby, and his son, Amon Henry Wilds, designed most of the best Regency buildings in Brighton. Amon Wilds was born in 1762 and started life as a builder in Lewes. He had some connection there with Thomas Read Kemp, who also originated from Lewes. This connection brought Wilds to Brighton, where he designed for Kemp a chapel which subsequently became Holy Trinity church, Ship Street, and may have built Kemp's own house, the Temple, in Montpelier Road. He transferred his office to Brighton in about 1815 and built as his own speculation the terraces known as Richmond Place and Waterloo Place (the latter since demolished) and possibly designed Regency Square. Then in 1822 Wilds entered into partnership with Charles Augustus Busby. Together they designed and built the original Kemp Town and Brunswick Town, as well as a lot of individual houses in Brighton. In fact, together with Wilds's son, Amon Henry Wilds, they were more responsible than anyone else for the special Regency character which Brighton has had ever since their time. Amon Wilds died in Brighton on 12 September 1833. His tomb was obviously designed by his son, Amon Henry Wilds, as it is surmounted by a shell – a form of ornamentation which Amon Henry Wilds frequently used in the tympana of windows in Brighton buildings such as the Royal Albion Hotel and Oriental Place. The inscription on the tomb had become illegible but fortunately was recorded in Erredge's *History of Brighton*. The Regency Society of Brighton and Hove had it relettered about twenty years ago. It is so badly worded that it is not without interest:

> A remarkable incident accompanies the period at which this gentleman came to Brighton. Through his abilities and taste the order of the ancient architecture of buildings in Brighton may be dated to have changed from its antiquated simplicity and rusticity; and its improvements have since progressively increased. He was a man of extensive genius, and in his reputation for uprightness of conduct could only meet its parallel.

Towards the southern end of the church-yard to the west of the pathway from Dyke Road is the table-tomb of John Pocock, who was a well-known Brighton figure for fifty years. He was a sawyer by profession who after 1790 became the landlord of the Hen & Chickens Inn, later the Running Horse, in King Street. He was also clerk to the Chapel Royal from 1785 to 1808, but is better known as clerk to the parish church from 1808 to 1846. His inscription says that 'in the discharge of his duty, how simple, upright and affectionate he was will alone be known at the last day. He came to his grave on the 13th June 1846 like a shock of corn cometh in his season, aged 81.' His function as parish clerk for thirty-eight years made him well-enough known for him to be the subject of a portrait print, a copy of which is in the Brighton Museum and which was reproduced in *Brighton Town and Brighton People* by Antony Dale, 1976. He is also commemorated by a small stained-glass window at the west end of the north aisle of St Nicholas's church, which was erected by his daughter, Mary Buckman, as late as 1880.

At the north end of the pathway from Dyke Road and opposite the south door of the church is the church-yard cross. The stepped base is medieval in date but the shaft was erected in 1934. The lantern at the summit with figures of the Crucifixion, the Virgin and Child, St Nicholas and St George was designed by Walter Godfrey, FSA, and carved by David Burns Brown.

Across the pathway to the west of the cross and immediately south of the doorway into the church is the latest memorial to be erected in the church-yard. This commemorates the actress Dame Flora Robson (1902–84) who lived at 7 Wykeham Terrace, which adjoins the church-yard on the south.

By the beginning of the nineteenth century the old church-yard was completely full. An extension to the north of Church Street was therefore opened in 1824 and has this date on the keystone over the entrance. This is now a children's playground. In 1832 the parish accepted a gift from George Lowdell of a small piece of land to the east of the pathway from Church Hill (now Dyke Road). This is recorded in a small tablet on the wall adjoining Wykeham Terrace. But neither of these extensions offered a permanent solution to the problem. So in 1841 a further burial-ground was opened to the west of Church Hill. This was laid out in ornamental fashion by Amon Henry Wilds and was originally intended to have included a stepped pyramid and catacombs, as in Highgate Cemetery, London. But a row on the subject blew up in the Vestry, and the elaborate work was never carried out. The entrance archway was erected in 1846, as is recorded on it.

One famous person, Sir Martin Archer Shee, PRA, was buried in this extension of the burial-ground. Shee was the son of a Dublin merchant. He was born in 1769 and became a pupil of Robert Lucius West at the Royal Dublin Society. His success as a portrait painter in Dublin led him to move to London in 1788. After a bad start there he was introduced to Sir Joshua Reynolds and Edmund Burke, and his pictures then found acceptance at the Royal Academy. He became an associate in 1798 and a royal academician in 1800. When Sir Thomas Lawrence died in 1830 Shee was elected president and received a knighthood. He was a very successful portrait painter, although never of the first rank. He also published poems, a tragedy and two novels. This entry into two art forms brought him the approval of no less a person than Lord Byron who, in 'English Bards and Scotch Reviewers' wrote: 'And here let Shee and genius find a place/Whose pen and pencil yield an equal grace.'

He was president of the Royal Academy for twenty years. He died in Brighton on 19 August 1850. Unfortunately, when this western extension of St Nicholas's church-yard was landscaped by Brighton Council after the Second World War Sir Martin Archer Shee's tomb was not respected and so cannot now be identified. But his tombstone can be seen in the centre of the western wall.

In 1869 the original church-yard was replanted with trees. This is recorded in a small tablet on the wall adjoining Wykeham Terrace. By the end of the Second World War the church-yard was in a very bad state. Many of the tombstones were damaged. In about 1960 Brighton Council relandscaped the land, removed some of the tombs and repaired others. All the historic monuments were left in their original positions and have since been relettered where necessary by the Regency Society and, in the case of Amon Wilds's tomb, protected by an iron railing.

Several of the incumbents of St Nicholas's church were men of mark. The Rev. Henry Michell was vicar from 1744 to 1789. He was the son of a Lewes attorney and was born in that town in 1715. He entered Clare College, Cambridge, in 1732, graduated BA in 1735 and MA in 1739, and was a fellow of the College from 1738 to 1740. In 1739 he became vicar of Maresfield in Sussex, and five years later was presented to the living of Brighthelmston. He held this in plurality with Maresfield. During the forty-five years that he occupied the living he presided over the transformation of Brighthelmston from a small fishing town to a full-dress seaside resort. He was friendly with all the distinguished people who began to frequent the place, such as the Thrales. This led him on one occasion into controversy with Dr Johnson. Michell was as vehement a Whig as Johnson was a Tory. One evening at a ball in the assembly rooms while the rest of the company were dancing Michell and Johnson were sitting by the fire in conversation. Their discussion became so heated that Michell seized the poker and Johnson the tongs. Both began thumping on the fender to emphasise their points. The ladies present had to prevail upon the master of ceremonies, Captain Wade, to intervene and separate the disputants.

The vicarage in Nile Street was at this time probably the largest house in Brighton. It was housed in part of what had been St Bartholomew's priory, as it is sometimes called, but was actually a grange or offshoot of St Pancras's priory at Southover, Lewes. Michell received pupils there as a young gentlemen's academy. One of his last pupils, in the years 1784–5, was the young Arthur Wellesley who was to become the first Duke of Wellington. Henry Michell died on 31 October 1789 and is buried in a vault under St Nicholas's church. A memorial to him was erected south of the tower archway on the west wall of the nave.

Henry Michell's successor, the Rev. Thomas Hudson, was vicar from 1789 to 1804. His incumbency was notable for two events. In 1790 he pulled down the medieval building which housed the vicarage and replaced it by a cobble-fronted Georgian house of three storeys. This remained the Brighton vicarage until 1835. Secondly, Hudson erected at his own expense the first chapel of ease in Brighton: the Chapel Royal, which was built between 1793 and 1795.

Thomas Hudson's successor was the Rev. Dr Robert James Carr. He was the son of the Rev. Colston Carr, a schoolmaster at Twickenham who became vicar of Ealing. R. J. Carr was born in 1774 and educated at Worcester College, Oxford. He married as early as 1797 and was ordained in the following year. He graduated as MA in 1806 and became a Doctor of Divinity in 1820. He was presented to the Brighton living in 1804. In 1820 he became Dean of Hereford also. He held both offices in plurality but always resided in Brighton during the summer, although not in the vicarage as this was occupied by one of the curates.

In 1824 Carr was promoted to the bishopric of Chichester. Plurality seems to have been a speciality of his as he held the bishopric jointly with a canonry of St Paul's Cathedral. At some time after his arrival at Brighton he became friendly with the Prince of Wales, afterwards George IV. The *Dictionary of National Biography* says that his 'eloquence commended him' to the Prince. But as the latter was not much of an attender at church and disliked sermons unless they gave him 'pleasure and satisfaction' (*George IV* by Christopher Hibbert, 1973), the connection is likely to have had a wider basis. At any rate during George IV's final illness Dr Carr stayed in Windsor Castle and administered the Sacrament to the King in his room. He also held the post of clerk to the Closet, which he retained during the next reign. The *Dictionary of National Biography* again says that he was dismissed on Queen Victoria's accession because of 'a strict adherence to his political principles'. But this is difficult to understand as he was not much involved in politics except that,

4 The Rev. H. M. Wagner, Vicar of Brighton 1824–70

being of the Evangelical school of thought, he was one of the bishops who voted against Catholic emancipation in 1829.

In 1831, probably as the result of a promise from the late King, he was translated to the see of Worcester and held that office until his death from paralysis in 1841, aged 67. There is a portrait of him in Hartlebury castle, the palace of the Bishops of Worcester, where he died.

Dr Carr's successor as Vicar of Brighton, the Rev. Henry Michell Wagner, was the most important man to hold the living of Brighton, not only on account of the long period through which he ministered there (1824–70) but also because of his character and achievements in the parish. He was the grandson of his predecessor, Henry Michell, and was born in 1792. He was educated at Eton and King's College, Cambridge, of which he was a fellow from 1815 to 1824. In 1817, on the recommendation of the Provost of Eton, Dr Joseph Goodall, he became tutor to the Duke of Wellington's two sons. When Dr Carr became Bishop of Chichester, presentation to the Brighton living, which normally rested with the Bishop of Chichester of the time, was made by the Crown in this instance. The Duke of Wellington, who was Master General of the Ordnance in Lord Liverpool's government, offered the incumbency to Wagner. The living was then worth £150 a year, plus another £150 for the parish of West Blatchington which had been united with the benefice in 1744.

When Wagner took office in 1824 there were only three Anglican churches in the town and three chapels of ease in course of construction. Two more were begun soon afterwards. All these, except for the parish church, were intended for the use of fashionable residents or visitors. Wagner immediately set himself to build, partly at his own expense and that of his family, a new series of churches intended for the inhabitants of the poorer districts of Brighton. These were: All Souls, Eastern Road (opened in 1838 and demolished in 1968); Christ Church, Montpelier Road (opened in 1838 and demolished in 1982); St John the Evangelist's, Carlton Hill (opened in 1840 and still standing but no longer in use as an Anglican church); St Paul's, West Street (opened in 1848); All Saints, Compton Road (opened in 1852 and demolished in 1957); and St Anne's, Burlington Street (opened in 1863 and demolished in 1986). Time has not been kind to these six churches of H. M. Wagner as only one of them (St Paul's) is still in use as an Anglican church. Wagner also built a new vicarage in Montpelier Road, to which he moved in 1835. The old vicarage was sold and demolished two years later.

In running the domestic affairs of St Nicholas's church Wagner had a very stormy passage. This was due partly to the fact that he had, except in ecclesiological matters, a difficult personality and partly to the fact that he held views which were unpopular in Brighton at that time. He was a high Tory when Brighton was largely Whig and even Radical. In addition the subject of compulsory church rates provided a perpetual bone of contention in a town which contained a large number of Dissenters. The full story of his battles with the Brighton Vestry is related in *The Wagners of Brighton* by Anthony Wagner and Antony Dale, 1983. However, after St Nicholas's church had been restored in 1853 on a voluntary basis matters became easier, and the last seventeen years of Wagner's incumbency were fairly peaceful. He died in the Brighton vicarage on 7 October 1870. He was buried in the Lewes Road cemetery, and his funeral was probably the grandest that Brighton had known up to that time. In addition, a memorial to him was erected on the west wall of St Nicholas's church to the north of the tower arch. Nine years after Wagner's death a stained-glass window in his memory was inserted in the westernmost window on the south side of the chancel. This was given by the vicar's life-long friend, Somers Clarke, and was designed by Charles Eamer Kempe. St Martin's church, Lewes Road, was also built in H. M. Wagner's memory by his three sons, but this is recorded in full in chapter 18.

H. M. Wagner's successor as vicar of Brighton in 1870 was the Rev. John Hannah. He was born in 1818 and educated at Christ Church, Oxford, where he took a first in classics. In 1840 he became a fellow of Lincoln College, Oxford, but after seven years there passed on to be rector of the Edinburgh Academy. In 1854 he became warden of Trinity College, Glenalmond, and Pantorian Professor of Theology. While there he was invited to give the Bampton lecture at Oxford in 1863.

When H. M. Wagner came to Brighton in 1824 there were only three Anglican places of worship in operation. At his death in 1870 there were eighteen. The presentation to most of these livings rested, after an initial period of forty years, with the vicar of Brighton. It is not surprising, therefore, that a contemporary Bishop of Chichester called Brighton 'a bishopric within a bishopric'. As a result, in 1873 the Bishop of Chichester, Dr Richard Durnford, with the cooperation of John Hannah, reorganised the whole parish of Brighton and allotted a district or parish to each church. The two churches of St Nicholas's and St Peter's were then separated, each being given a parish. The status of the parish church was transferred from St Nicholas's to St Peter's, presumably as being the more central building of the two. John Hannah then gave up the charge of St Nicholas's.

When John Hannah came to Brighton his son, the Rev. John Julius Hannah, came with him. The latter was born in 1843 and educated at Trinity College, Glenalmond and Balliol College, Oxford. He was ordained at Cuddesdon Theological College, Oxfordshire. His first curacies were at Maidenhead (1867–70) and Paddington (1870–1). On coming to Brighton he was at first curate to his father and was put in charge of St Nicholas's church. When this church was separated from St Peter's in 1873 John Julius Hannah was presented to be vicar of St Nicholas's and held the living until 1888.

One later incumbent of St Nicholas's needs to be mentioned. This was the Rev. Hugh Maudsley Hordern, who was vicar from 1910 to 1924. From 1923 to 1929 he was Archdeacon of Lewes and from 1929 until his death in 1946 Suffragan Bishop of Lewes.

2

THE CHAPEL ROYAL

In 1750 Dr Richard Russell published his famous book *De Tabe Glandulari* which advocated sea-bathing for the treatment of swellings of the glands of the throat. By the 1780s fashionable visitors were coming to Brighton in large numbers. These included in 1783 George Prince of Wales. As a result, the parish church of St Nicholas became uncomfortably crowded. The Rev. Thomas Hudson, who was appointed vicar of Brighton in 1789, decided to build an additional chapel for the accommodation of this company. He may also have had in mind the fact that the Prince of Wales, who was not famous for church attendance, had put in very few appearances at the parish church, which was some distance away from the Royal Pavilion. If Hudson built another place of worship very near to the Prince's house the Prince would have little excuse for not attending services there. The vicar consulted the Prince, who proved very cooperative. He agreed to rent a pew, and on 25 November 1793 with full masonic honours laid the foundation stone of the new chapel in what was to become Prince's Place, North Street, Brighton. The architect was Thomas Saunders of Upper James Street, Golden Square, London (who died in 1798). The builder was named Bodle. The work was completed in just over a year. The first service was held in the chapel on 3 August 1795 in the presence of the newly-married Prince and Princess of Wales.

Architecturally, the new chapel was a simple classical building with only one elevation exposed, facing east. This was faced with stucco and had round-headed sash windows. Above the three centre first-floor windows was a truncated pediment surmounted by the Royal arms. Along the ground floor was a colonnade of Doric columns. When first built the chapel was separated from North Street by a shop with a dwelling over it. This had a very handsome curved shop-front of many panes.

5 The original Chapel Royal. Drawing by W. A. Delamotte

Inside, the chapel was a typical Georgian preaching-house with galleries on all four sides. These galleries were supported on columns with capitals in the form of the Prince of Wales's feathers. In Delamotte's drawing of the interior they look something like the columns in the kitchen of the Royal Pavilion, which are meant to simulate palm trees. The chapel was the first of many Brighton churches to be wrongly orientated. The altar was at the west end. The gallery above, which contained the organ, was decorated with the Royal arms and the Prince of Wales's feathers. There was an elaborate three-decker pulpit with a curved staircase leading up to it. This was the first of many elaborate pulpits which were a dominant feature of all early nineteenth-century Brighton churches. They have unfortunately been swept away since by Tractarian and later reforms. There is only one such pulpit

6 The interior of the original Chapel Royal. Drawing by W. A. Delamotte

remaining in the whole diocese of Chichester. This is at St John's church, Chichester, by James Elmes (1812). The church is now closed and in the hands of the Redundant Churches Fund.

During its first years the Chapel Royal was served by the vicar of Brighton and his curates but was only used during the fashionable season. Sacred concerts were also held there. This was a tradition that was continued for many years at the Chapel Royal. Singers as famous as Madame Catalani gave their services. The Prince of Wales's band often took part. Similarly, when well-known preachers took part in the services the collections that were taken for charities often reached considerable sums.

Thomas Hudson, however, felt a financial strain in running the chapel and mortgaged it for £800 in 1794, for £1,200 in 1796 and for £800 in 1799. In 1803 Hudson thought that it was necessary to put the chapel on a more formal basis. He therefore obtained a private Act of Parliament to constitute it as an official chapel of ease to the parish church. This act was the prototype of all the subsequent private Acts of Parliament which were granted for later chapels of ease in Brighton. It empowered Hudson and his successors in title as vicars of Brighton to nominate in perpetuity a perpetual curate for appointment by the Bishop of Chichester and to set aside sufficient pews to produce an income of £115 a year for the stipend of such a curate. Out of this sum the curate was required to pay the salary of a clerk and to provide bread and wine for the Communion. Fees for baptisms and funerals had to be paid in duplicate to the curate and to the vicar of Brighton. The building was not licensed for the celebration of marriages. Two hundred and twenty-four free seats were provided. Thomas Hudson was authorised to sell or rent the remainder of the pews to the highest bidders. Such lettings carried with them the obligation to share in the burden of any repairs that the chapel had subsequently to undergo. An admission charge of one shilling a head was made to visitors who did not buy or rent a pew.

Hudson was also empowered to let the vaults below the chapel. These were leased to a wine merchant, which produced the quip:

> There's a Spirit above and a Spirit below:
> The Spirit of bliss and the Spirit of woe.
> The Spirit above is the Spirit Divine;
> The Spirit below is the Spirit of wine.

The Chapel Royal, with this official title, was consecrated on 16 August 1803 by the Bishop of Chichester, Dr John Buckner. The Prince of Wales was not present. His attendance in fact had not lasted very long. It is said that on one occasion a sermon by a curate, the Rev. W. Brook, on the text of 'Thou art the man' offended him, and he never returned to worship there. But he retained his pew, although the rent was not always paid without a reminder being sent. Later, when the Castle Hotel was demolished, the King – as by then he had become – bought the building and converted the ballroom into his private chapel. Thus his connection with the Chapel Royal ceased altogether. But other members of the Royal family continued to attend services at the Chapel Royal from time to time, such as the Duke and Duchess of Gloucester in 1825. The last member to do so was George IV's sister, Princess Augusta, in 1840.

Thomas Hudson resigned the vicarage of Brighton in 1804 but he continued to minister at the Chapel Royal for another four years and was appointed its first official perpetual curate. He sold the freehold of the building in

1805 to the Rev. William Peckham Woodward for £2,000. When Hudson resigned the perpetual curacy of the Chapel Royal in 1808 the new vicar of Brighton, the Rev. Dr Robert James Carr, nominated Woodward as perpetual curate, but the Bishop of Chichester refused to accept the nomination. Hudson's actual successor was therefore the Rev. John Portis. Carr and Portis then proceeded to acquire from William Woodward the freehold of the building between them in equal shares. Portis remained at the Chapel Royal until 1814, when he is said to have left 'under a cloud'.

The most important of the early perpetual curates of the Chapel Royal was the Rev. Thomas Trocke who was appointed in 1834 after serving for two years as a curate at St Nicholas's church. He remained in charge until 1875. During that time he managed to acquire five-eighths of the freehold of the building. In 1848 a lantern light was inserted in the chapel. At the same time £200 was subscribed by the congregation as a tribute to Thomas Trocke, which was used to provide a chandelier below the lantern light, together with a piece of plate for his personal use. In the reorganisation of the parish of Brighton which took place in 1873 the Chapel Royal was assigned a district of its own.

On Thomas Trocke's retirement the chapel was found to be in bad repair. The colonnade along the east front had been demolished, and some of the windows had been altered. The liturgical arrangements of 1795 were no longer acceptable in a post-Tractarian world. So it was decided to refurbish the interior, and the chapel was closed from June 1876 to February 1877. The remodelling was entrusted to Arthur Blomfield – a competent architect who was knighted in 1889 but was never of the top rank. Since the revival of interest in Victorian architecture he has never aroused the enthusiasm that has been shown for such contemporaries as G. F. Bodley or G. E. Street. The work cost £2,700. The builders were G. Lynn & Sons.

The west gallery over the altar was removed and enough land acquired to form a small chancel. This was separated from the nave by an elegant iron screen on a wooden base, with a new pulpit and lectern in front of it. The old pulpit was given to St Stephen's church. Although galleries were out of fashion in 1876, the other three galleries were retained but given new open-work balustrades. In the process the Royal pew and the Royal arms were removed, although the arms were reinstated in 1926. A new ceiling was inserted and Thomas Trocke's chandelier taken down. The box-pews were all replaced.

Archdeacon John Hannah, who had become vicar of Brighton on H. M. Wagner's death in 1870, disapproved of private proprietory rights in churches, so he bought out the proprietors of the Chapel Royal (Thomas Trocke five-eighths, R. Cox a quarter and R. Tiltstone one-eighth) for £2,000. The free sittings were extended by redeeming some of the pew rents. But these were not finally extinguished until 1896.

In all this work no thought was given to rebuilding the exterior of the chapel. But in 1880 an unexpected event occurred. The houses along the North Street frontage of the chapel were demolished. This revealed the south elevation of the chapel which was never meant to be seen. Blomfield was therefore commissioned to design a new exterior. He produced a plan with a tower at the south-east corner. But this tower was to stand on land belonging to Brighton Council, who were unwilling to give this for the purpose and turned down the plans. Blomfield then produced a design without a tower. But the reaction to this was so unfavourable that he was commissioned to make yet a third design, again with a tower. After pressure was exerted on the Council they eventually agreed to make a gift of the necessary land for the tower.

The cost was to be £1,200, so it was decided to confine the work for the time being to the replacement of the south elevation only. The work on the east elevation was to be postponed for four years, but it was actually thirteen years before it was completed. Blomfield's new design for this was not much more than a slightly grandiose version in red brick of Saunder's original elevation with a larger pediment. The main virtue of the new building was and is the clock-tower which is a notable feature of the street-scape and provides the emphasis which so many Brighton churches lack because their projected towers were never built.

In 1896 the Rev. Seymour Penzer became perpetual curate of the chapel. He paid off the mortgage of £800 remaining from the rebuilding of 1881, redeemed the few surviving pew rents and obtained an Order in Council which allotted a formal parish to the church. At his request the Rev. John Julius Hannah, who had succeeded his father, Archdeacon Hannah, as vicar of Brighton in 1888, conveyed the freehold of the building to the Ecclesiastical Commissioners. But strangely enough Hannah refused to include in the transfer the vaults below the chapel which were let for the storage of wine. These brought him in a small income which was the equivalent of interest on the sum of £2,000 that his father had expended in buying the chapel.

7 The Chapel Royal 1987

Seymour Penzer died in 1918, and a screen round the pulpit and chancel
was erected in his memory in the following year.

By the early years of the twentieth century the old centre of Brighton
had become largely commercial, and few residents remained in the area that
formed the parish of the Chapel Royal. In 1921, 1928 and 1930 consideration
was given to amalgamation of the church with Holy Trinity, Ship Street.
The latter did not have a parish of its own but was so near to the Chapel
Royal that it was also affected by the commercialisation of the district. But
agreement was not reached on any of these occasions. After the Second World
War the congregation diminished still further, and the Chapel Royal was
eventually united with the parish church of St Peter's. The south aisle was

converted into a bookshop for the Society for the Propagation of Christian Knowledge. When Holy Trinity church came to be closed in 1984 an arrangement was made for special services for its former congregation to be held at the Chapel Royal.

3

ST PETER'S CHURCH
(the parish church)

The third Anglican church to be opened in Brighton was St James's in St James's Street. This was first built in 1810–13 and was intended as a chapel of ease to the parish church. But the curate proposed for it had not met the approval of the vicar of Brighton, Dr Robert James Carr. The proprietors therefore had no choice but to run it as a dissenting chapel. In 1817 it was bought by Nathaniel Kemp of Ovingdean Hall, the uncle of Thomas Read Kemp, and converted for Anglican services. Later, in 1826, it was placed on a regular basis by a private Act of Parliament. It was rebuilt in 1875 by the local architect, Edmund Scott, and demolished as redundant a hundred years later.

By 1818 the population of Brighton was 18,000. Even with the opening of St James's chapel it was clear that the accommodation in Anglican churches was inadequate to the demand for seats, particularly for free sittings. Consequently on 5 November 1818 a meeting of the Brighton Vestry resolved that another church should be built as an official chapel of ease to St Nicholas's. As that year had already seen the passing of an Act of Parliament setting up a national body of commissioners for the building of additional churches, the parish decided to proceed under the aegis of that Act, rather than obtain a special local Act of Parliament. The cost was to be paid partly out of the parish poor-rate and partly out of voluntary subscriptions. The Commissioners for Building New Churches agreed to make a loan of £15,000 as a charge on the rates, repayable in annual instalments of £1,500. Thomas Read Kemp undertook to act as honorary treasurer of the appeal, and the trustees appointed were Lord Egremont, the Lord Lieutenant of Sussex, Sir David Scott and the vicar of Brighton.

A competition for the design of the building was organised. This was won

8 St Peter's church as originally designed by Sir Charles Barry

by Charles Barry, a then quite unknown architect who had just returned
from a grand tour, not only of Italy but also of Greece and Turkey. The
church was more or less his first commission, but at almost the same moment
he was successful in the competition to build the original portion of the Sussex
County Hospital in Brighton. The runners-up in the competition for St
Peter's were the local partnership, Amon Wilds and Charles Augustus Busby,
who were then building Kemp Town and Brunswick Town in Brighton.
The contract for building the church was given to William Ranger.

The foundation stone was laid by the vicar of Brighton, Dr Robert James
Carr, on 8 May 1824. A procession, headed by a band, went from the Old
Ship Hotel to the site in the Valley Gardens, pausing opposite Dr Carr's
house in Grand Parade to play the national anthem. In the evening a dinner
was held to mark the occasion at the Old Ship Hotel.

The Vestry invited local stone quarries to supply samples of stone available.
But this evidently did not produce any satisfactory result for the church was

built of Portland stone. The Gothic revival was in its early stages so that Barry was able to use the Perpendicular style which so stupidly came to be despised by later architects like Sir Gilbert Scott but which has produced many fine nineteenth-century churches. St Peter's is orientated from north to south with the tower rather unusually forming a porch at the south end. But it is so well-sited that the gleaming white stone of the tower catches the full force of the sun across the gardens to the south. The north end of the church as first built had an apsidal projection which contained the vestry. Barry originally intended that the tower should be surmounted by a spire and as late as 1841 expressed regret that this spire had not been built. But if one looks at the various prints of the church showing the intended spire it is difficult to think that this would have added much to the general effect. There is no explanation of why the spire was not built, but this was almost certainly on account of the cost involved. Even without the spire the church is one of the finest early Gothic revival churches in England and the first great nineteenth-century Brighton church.

The church-yard round the church was planted with a number of trees that all had symbolic religious significance. But these have gradually been replaced over the years by the more ordinary elm and sycamore.

Barry's estimate for building the church was £14,703. 9s. 6d. Finance soon began to give trouble. This was due to the objection by non-Anglican residents to the payment of compulsory church rates which were used for building and maintaining Anglican churches. As a result the Vestry was determined throughout the whole process of building not to exceed the sum of £15,000 originally contemplated. In 1824 the Vestry applied to the Commissioners for Building New Churches for further help and were given a grant of £3,000, to be deducted from the loan of £15,000 which had to be repaid. But a subsequent disagreement arose over this which led to the issue of a writ of mandamus for the repayment of this sum. In 1827 an application for a further grant was refused, but the Commissioners agreed that part of the debt which the parish had incurred should be repaid out of the income from pew rents. When the church accounts were published in 1828 these showed a total expenditure of £20,365. 5s. But the parish claimed that their original vote of £15,000 had not been exceeded. So it looks as if the balance of nearly £5,000, apart from whatever was received in voluntary contributions, must have come from grants from the Commissioners for Building New Churches.

9 The east end of the original interior of St Peter's church. Drawing by W. A. Delamotte

In 1827 the Vestry voted a special sum of £1,500 for the internal fittings of the church, including an external clock in the tower to be illuminated by gas. But when they paid the architect's fee of £1,150. 13s. they refused to pay an additional amount of £45 for designing the organ-case and £13 for alterations to the west gallery. They also asked Barry to hand over the working drawings of the church, which he refused to do as being contrary to custom.

Externally St Peter's was a forward-looking building of the nineteenth century, even in advance of its time. Internally the atmosphere of the eighteenth century predominated. There were three large galleries. The south (liturgical west) gallery, which later had the Royal arms fixed to it, had an upper gallery above it and the organ behind that. There were box pews throughout, finished with Gothic detail. The most prominent objects were a pair of pulpits with curved staircases flanking the aisle. One was for conducting the service, the other for preaching the sermon. These balancing pulpits were the first example of what was to become a common feature in early nineteenth-century Brighton churches. There was originally no chancel at St Peter's, and the terminal feature of the north (liturgical east) end was a plaster Gothic screen with four panels of texts flanked by canopied niches. On each side of the niches were doorways which led into the vestry that occupied the apse. The ceiling consisted of plaster vaulting. The painted windows in the clerestory were given by the new vicar, the Rev. H. M. Wagner, or by members of his family. The church plate was the gift of the Lord Lieutenant of Sussex, Lord Egremont.

The church seated 1,800 people. The Commissioners for Building New Churches had insisted as a condition of their grants and loan that a large number of free seats should be provided. There were originally to have been 1,100 of these, but under pressure from the parish the Commissioners agreed to this number being reduced to 900. Some pews were set aside to provide a stipend of £150 a year for the perpetual curate and £50 for the clerk, although it is doubtful whether the curate ever received as much money as that. The remainder of the pews were let in the usual manner, in the first instance to repay the debt incurred in building the church.

St Peter's was opened for the first time on 24 January 1828 for a sacred concert. This was attended by Princess Augusta, the King's sister. The church was consecrated on the following day by the Bishop of Chichester who, as vicar of Brighton, had laid the foundation stone in 1824.

The first perpetual curate, who was responsible for operation of the church under the supervision of the vicar, H. M. Wagner, was the Rev. Thomas Cooke. He was born in 1791 and ordained in 1813. He served as a chaplain in the army during the last part of the Peninsular War and at the battle of Waterloo. These Wellingtonian connections must have introduced him to Henry Wagner, who made him one of his curates a year before St Peter's was opened. He ministered at St Peter's during the whole period of Wagner's incumbency and only resigned in 1872 in order to facilitate the reorganisation of the whole parish, which was carried out in the following year by Wagner's successor and the Bishop of Chichester. Throughout the period from 1827 to 1870 Thomas Cooke was Wagner's closest associate in all the affairs of the parish and read the office at Wagner's funeral. On Thomas Cooke's retirement in 1872 he was presented with a model of St Peter's church in silver. One wonders what has become of this model. Cooke died on 18 December 1874, aged 83. The font at St Peter's was given in his memory, and a tablet to him can be seen on the south wall of the church.

The death of Henry Michell Wagner in 1870 and the retirement of Thomas Cooke in 1872 began a new epoch in the history of St Peter's church. The new vicar of Brighton was the Rev. John Hannah. He and the Bishop of Chichester, Dr Richard Durnford, reorganised the whole parish of Brighton, as has already been mentioned in the previous chapter. St Nicholas's and St Peter's were separated, and by order in Council St Peter's became the parish church. John Hannah's son, the Rev. John Julius Hannah, took over the care of St Nicholas's from his father.

By that time St Peter's was nearly fifty years old. The fabric was beginning to need attention. Although the church nominally seated 1,800, in actual fact it only provided accommodation for about half that number because some of the pews, particularly in the galleries, were so cramped that it was impossible to kneel in them. The possibility of exit in case of fire was quite inadequate. The heating and ventilation systems needed overhauling. The vicar therefore called a public meeting at the Town Hall on 21 May 1874. At this Somers Clarke, who was clerk to the Vestry, presented two alternative plans for alterations to the building on behalf of his son of the same name who had been a pupil of Sir Gilbert Scott. The first of these was for general repairs amounting to about £3,000. The second was more ambitious and proposed the expenditure of about £16,000 for work which would have included the removal of the south (liturgical west) gallery, the provision of a chancel and the extension of the nave by one bay. The vicar at first said that he was not inclined to take on the task of raising £16,000 by public subscription. But after he had been called faint-hearted by other speakers and had realised that much support was available he agreed to the passing of a resolution in favour of the larger sum. In fact he went further. Mindful of the fact that in the 1853 restoration of the then parish church (St Nicholas's) H. M. Wagner, as vicar of Brighton, had given £1,000 towards the total sum of £4,948 which was raised, John Hannah offered to give £500 in the first place and £250 a year for the two years following. To this Somers Clarke senior added a gift of £100. But not all the work then contemplated was in fact carried out at the time. No real chancel was built for another twenty-five years. But a new stone reredos with canopied niches was inserted in the place of Barry's original screen. This was designed by E. L. Blackburne and executed by J. W. Searle of Walworth. The whole church was reseated. Part only of the south (liturgical west) gallery was removed to accommodate the organ. The church was reopened for worship on 16 April 1876.

The insertion of stained-glass windows was not included in this work of 1874–7. But during the next decade a number of windows designed by Charles Eamer Kempe of Old Place, Lindfield, were placed in the church.

John Hannah became a prebendary of Chichester cathedral in 1874 and Archdeacon of Lewes in 1876. He held the latter office concurrently with the incumbency of Brighton until his death. His achievement in Brighton was not only that he reorganised the the whole parish but that, in the words of his memorial tablet, he 'made each district church free and unappropri-ated'. He died on 1 June 1888. A memorial tablet to him was erected on the east wall of St Peter's church.

John Hannah was succeeded as vicar of Brighton by his son, the Rev. John Julius Hannah, who had been in charge of St Nicholas's church since 1870. He immediately addressed himself to the problem of adding a chancel to St Peter's. He turned to the same architect, Somers Clarke, who by that time was in partnership with another of Sir Gilbert Scott's pupils, John Thomas Micklethwaite. They produced a plan not only for a chancel but also for a chapel to the east (liturgical south) of it. Work was begun first on the chapel, and its foundation stone was laid by the Bishop of Chichester, Dr Richard Durnford, in 1889. The chapel was completed in 1898 but the chancel took another eight years. John Julius Hannah did not remain in Brighton long enough to see this chancel finished, for he became Dean of

10 St Peter's church 1987

Chichester in 1902. He held that office for twenty-seven years, resigning in 1929 at the age of 86. He died two years later.

The completion of the addition at St Peter's fell to Hannah's successor as vicar of Brighton, Canon Benedict George Hoskyns (1902–17). The chancel and east (liturgical south) chapel were consecrated on 29 June 1906 by the Bishop of Chichester, Dr E. R. Wilberforce, in the presence of the Archbishop of Canterbury, Dr Randall Davidson. The mayor of Brighton was also present and gave an official lunch party in the Royal Pavilion after the ceremony. The chancel and chapel are built of sandstone, which does not match with the Portland stone of the nave. The additions are also in Perpendicular style but rather heavier than the original building. The builders were Norman & Burt and the cost, presumably of the chancel only, was £8,000.

A new reredos in Flemish Gothic was designed by W. H. Randall Blacking. The chief feature of the new building is probably the north (liturgical east) window of the chancel. This was designed by Charles Eamer Kempe and is one of the largest and finest windows that ever came out of his studio. It was erected in memory of Queen Victoria. A portrait of the Queen herself appears in the right-hand bottom corner. At the same time as the chancel was added the three galleries were removed from the nave. With their removal the atmosphere of the church passed from the eighteenth to the nineteenth century.

Another item of royal association is the organ which was given in 1910 in memory of King Edward VII and installed in the church. But the case was not made until 1966. At that date the whole church underwent a thorough restoration costing £25,000 under the supervision of John Leopold Denman. The design of the organ-case was his work. Brighton Council contributed £10,000 towards this restoration. The painting of the chancel ceiling formed part of the work done then. The 'Jesse' window by Hugh Easton in the west aisle of the nave was inserted slightly earlier.

In 1828 two bells were given to St Peter's from St Nicholas's. Six were added later. But in 1914 these were replaced by a peal of ten bells, which gives the church good ringing status.

Several later vicars of Brighton achieved preferment on or after leaving Brighton. Dr Frederick Cyril Nugent Hicks (1924–7) was Bishop of Gibraltar from 1927 to 1933 and subsequently Bishop of Lincoln. His successor, Canon Alfred Casey Wollaston Rose, went on to become Suffragan Bishop of Dover in 1935. The next vicar, the Rev. John Charles Halland How (1933–8) became Bishop of Glasgow and Gallaway in 1938 and Primus of Scotland in 1946. His successor, Canon Geoffrey Hodgson Warde (1939–44), left to become canon and Archdeacon of Carlisle but returned to Sussex in 1945 as Suffragan Bishop of Lewes.

4

ST GEORGE'S CHURCH

During the 1820s the growth in the population of Brighton was greater than in any other decade of the nineteenth century. The increase was from 24,429 in 1821 to 40,634 in 1831. Most of the best Regency squares or terraces were built during this decade. The same rate of increase was reflected in the number of new churches that were built in the reign of George IV. In addition to St Peter's no less than four proprietory chapels were erected in Brighton during the decade, and one in the adjoining parish of Hove.

The first of these was St Margaret's church in Cannon Place. This was intended as the church for the newly built Regency Square. It was the enterprise of an extraordinary jack-of-all-trades named Barnard Gregory who was at one time or other chemist, wine merchant, banker, insurance broker, journalist, newspaper-proprietor and actor. His contributions to journalism were so scurrilous that, when he turned to acting, he was frequently hooted off the stage. The building of the church was entirely a financial speculation. It was only called St Margaret's because his wife's Christian name was Margaret. The foundation stone was laid by her on 15 May 1824. The design has always been attributed to the vague figure of Mr Clarke of London. But we now know that it was the work of Charles Augustus Busby as full working drawings signed by him have come to light amongst the collection of Busby drawings acquired by the Royal Institute of British Architects. It was completed in seven months and opened for worship on 26 December in the same year. In June 1825 Gregory obtained a private Act of Parliament to regularise the position of the church.

St Margaret's was an extremely attractive classical building. It had an elegant Ionic portico which formed the terminal feature of St Margaret's Place and a dome and lantern over the central portion with galleries on three

11 The original interior of St George's church. Drawing by W. A. Delamotte

sides and an additional upper gallery at the nave end. An unsuitable Roman-
esque chancel was added by J. Oldrid Scott in 1874. Despite this addition
St Margaret's was the best classical church in Brighton. It remained Evangelical in tradition throughout its life. It was most insensitively demolished by
the Chichester Diocesan Board of Finance in 1959. Neither Brighton Council
nor the Minister of Housing and Local Government was willing to intervene,
although the building could have been used to house the magnificent collection of historic costumes which had been offered to the town by Mrs Doris
Langley Moore. This collection consequently went to Bath instead.

Contemporaneously with St Margaret's another proprietory chapel – St
George's – was being built in Brighton. This was the enterprise of a very
different promoter from Barnard Gregory: Thomas Read Kemp. He was
born on 23 December 1782 at Barbican House, Lewes, where his family had

42

inherited property from prosperous merchants named Friend. He was the son of another Thomas Kemp, who was Member of Parliament for Lewes. He was educated at St John's College, Cambridge, where, most unusually, he read theology. He married Frances, daughter of the banker Sir Francis Baring, in 1806 and lived at Herstmonceux Place in Sussex and later at the Temple in Montpelier Road, Brighton. When his father died in 1811 he succeeded to his father's seat in Parliament. But in 1816 he separated himself from fashionable life, seceded from the Church of England and founded a dissenting sect of his own. For its use he built a chapel, first in Lewes and then in Brighton, at which he himself ministered. The Brighton chapel in due course became Holy Trinity church, Ship Street. But the sect did not last more than about seven years. Kemp himself returned to the Church of England and was again elected to Parliament.

In 1823 to recoup his diminished finances he embarked on his great architectural enterprise of building Kemp Town on the East Cliff at Brighton to the design of Amon Wilds and Charles Augustus Busby. For this estate a church was needed, as St Margaret's had been needed for Regency Square. For this purpose Kemp set himself to build St George's church. He obtained a private Act of Parliament. This was dated 3 June 1824 and in almost all respects followed the model of the Act of 1803 relating to the Chapel Royal. Kemp was empowered to appoint in perpetuity a perpetual curate and to set aside sufficient pew rents to provide his stipend of £150 a year. The remainder of the pews Kemp could sell or let for his own benefit in the usual way.

The architect of the church was Charles Augustus Busby, and the cost £11,000. The church was consecrated on 30 December 1825 by the Bishop of Chichester, Dr Robert James Carr, and opened for worship two days later.

St George's is a simple classical building of yellow brick with stucco dressings. The west end has a portico of paired Ionic and Doric columns, surmounted by a tower, into which a clock-face was inserted in 1840. Inside there are galleries on three sides. These are curved at the west end. Two elegant curved staircases in the narthex give access to the galleries. Originally the organ, which was built by the firm of Bishop, stood in the west gallery. There was no chancel and the reredos consisted of three panels of texts, with a pulpit of three tiers in front of them. The first perpetual curate, the Rev. George Siveright, only served for three years. In 1828 he was succeeded by the most important minister in the history of St George's, the Rev. James

12 The Rev. J. S. M. Anderson

Stuart Murray Anderson. He was born in Bombay on 22 October 1800 and educated at Balliol College, Oxford. In 1833 he was appointed chaplain in Ordinary to Queen Adelaide. Later he held the same appointment to Queen Victoria. Queen Adelaide, who was very pious, frequently attended the afternoon services at St George's. The Royal arms on the west gallery is a reminder of this association. As the result of the Queen's attendance St George's became so fashionable that an extra gallery was added at the west end in 1831. This is said to have been built by Thomas Cubitt's firm in one week. It was sometimes called the 'sky parlour' or the 'fishermen's gallery', although no fishermen can possibly have lived within about a mile of the church. To make way for this gallery the organ was moved to the east end, where it was most strangely placed immediately above and behind the altar. Queen Adelaide also marked her patronage of the church by giving the communion plate of two silver chalices, two patens and a flagon, which are the work of William Bateman and bear the date 1825.

In 1830 or 1831 Thomas Read Kemp sold the freehold and the right of presentation to St George's church to Lawrence Peel of 32 Sussex Square, Brighton, the youngest brother of Sir Robert Peel. He had married Lady Julia Lennox, daughter of the fourth Duke of Richmond. During his sixty years' residence in Brighton he played a most important part in the life of St George's church and was a prominent supporter of many charities in Brighton, particularly the Sussex County Hospital. Portraits of him and of Lady Jane Peel still hang in the boardroom of the hospital.

J. S. M. Anderson remained perpetual curate of St George's until 1851. He lived at 12 Arundel Terrace. These years were probably the most prominent period in the church's history, largely on account of Anderson's position in the town. He was the first chaplain of the Sussex County Hospital until 1835, a life governor and eventually chairman of the managing committee. He was the first honorary secretary of the Kemp Town Enclosures Committee and held that office for nineteen years. He was also a Town Commissioner. From 1844 to 1858 he was chaplain to Lincoln's Inn. As a preacher, he was described by Charles Greville as 'very eloquent, voice and manner perfect, one of the best I ever heard, both preacher and reader (*The Greville Memoirs*). He left Brighton in 1851 to become vicar of Tormonton in Gloucestershire.

His successor, the Rev. Jacob Hugo North ministered from 1851 to 1877. St George's was allotted a parish or district in 1879. Lady Jane Peel died in 1861, Lawrence Peel in 1888. They were both buried in a vault under the church. They and three of their children have memorials in the north-east corner of the nave.

The death of Lawrence Peel marked the end of an epoch in the history of St George's. In 1889 his son, Charles Lennox Peel, sold the freehold and the advowson of the church to the congregation for £4,000. They immediately vested this in the trustees of the Church Patronage Society, in whose hands it still remains. The congregation then set about bringing the church into line with the ecclesiastical ideas of the late nineteenth century by building a chancel. Charles Lennox Peel donated £1,000 towards this. The new addition was lit by a round-headed window of nondescript style. The north and south galleries were slightly extended to the east to be level with the new chancel. The new classical reredos very faithfully matched the spirit of the old one but was of five panels of texts instead of three. The organ was moved from behind the altar to the extended east end of the south gallery. The pulpit was also moved to its present position. Unfortunately the congregation did not content themselves with these additions but also made alterations

13 St George's church 1987

to the nave which were not an improvement. They replaced the wooden
or stuccoed columns of the galleries (Doric on the ground floor and Ionic
above) with thinner cast-iron columns with acanthus-leaved captals. The
solid fronts of the galleries were partly replaced by open-work and painted
deal. All the box-pews were removed, and the whole church reseated. As
so reseated, the church could accommodate 1,300 people. The total cost of
the work done from 1889 to 1890 was £11,050 which was exactly equal

46

to the original cost of the nave of 1824–5.

The result of this rebuilding is that the interior of St George's dates largely from the late nineteenth century. But the work was done so much in the style of sixty years before that the church still retains the atmosphere of an early nineteenth-century chapel of ease. This was probably due to the fact that at the time and indeed until very recently the traditions of the church remained Evangelical in character.

In 1962 an attempt was made by the Chichester diocesan authorities to close the church, and the suggestion was made of possibly converting it into a surplus bookstore for Brighton library. This was successfully resisted by the congregation and the Church Patronage Society. A few years later the church was united with the parish of St Anne's. That church dated from 1862–8 and was the sixth and last church to be built by the Rev. H. M. Wagner, as vicar of Brighton. It was designed by Benjamin Ferrey, who was a pupil of A. W. Pugin's but had no great character. Following the amalgamation the church was closed as redundant and demolished in 1986.

5

HOLY TRINITY CHURCH

Of the other two proprietory chapels built in Brighton during the 1820s, one had a double connection with St George's. This was Trinity chapel, which in due course became Holy Trinity church. As has already been mentioned, Thomas Read Kemp seceded from the Church of England in 1816 and founded his own dissenting sect. This met at first in Lewes. But in 1817 Kemp commissioned the Lewes builder and architect, Amon Wilds, to build him a chapel in Brighton in the part of Ship Street which was originally called Ship Street Lane. This building had a stuccoed elevation facing east with five round-headed windows on the first floor and a pediment over surmounted by a square tower. Immediately adjoining on the south and facing Duke Street was a handsome Georgian red-brick house, which was not demolished until 1867 when Duke Street was widened.

Inside, the chapel was lit by a glass dome under the tower. The chief feature of the interior was the pulpit which took the shape of a vase springing from a turned and fluted Ionic column. From this presumably the flower of dissenting eloquence could flow.

Kemp ministered at Trinity chapel until 1823, when he returned to orthodoxy. He was succeeded as minister by his friend and solicitor, George Faithful, of the firm of G. & H. Faithful of 15 Ship Street, Brighton. Faithful was later to become one of the first Members of Parliament for Brighton in 1833. In 1825, when St George's church was being built, Kemp sold the freehold of the Ship Street chapel to the Rev. Robert Anderson, who converted it for Anglican worship. Robert Anderson has been rather overshadowed by his better known brother, James, at St. George's church. Robert was the eldest son of Captain Robert Anderson of the East India Company Marine Service, who was also a ship-owner in his own right. He was born

14 The original Trinity chapel *c.* 1850

on 3 April 1792 and educated at the East Indian College at Hertford Castle which later moved to Haileybury. There he studied oriental languages. In 1810 he sailed for India as a writer to the East India Company. He was at first appointed assistant under-secretary in the Department of Revenue and Justice in Madras. Having become a fluent linguist, he was later appointed deputy translator in Persian to the Government of Madras and deputy registrar to the Civil and Criminal Courts of that province. In 1819 on account of ill health he returned to England and became assistant professor of oriental languages at Haileybury from 1820 to 1825. At this time he published two books on the Tamil language. His father's death enabled him to turn from oriental languages to the church. He was ordained deacon in 1821 and priest in the following year.

Anderson obtained a private Act of Parliament to place Trinity chapel on an official basis. This was dated 22 March 1826 and followed much the same pattern as the Acts relating to the Chapel Royal and St George's church, except that it empowered Anderson to appoint, with the approval of the vicar of Brighton and the Bishop of Chichester, a perpetual curate for only an initial period of forty years, after which period the right of presentation passed to the vicar of Brighton. The stipend was the usual £150 a year. As Anderson bought the building for his own use he presented himself to the living. The church was consecrated by the Bishop of Chichester, Dr R. J. Carr, on 21 April 1826.

Anderson commissioned Charles Barry, who was then working at St Peter's church, Brighton to 're-order', as it would now be termed, the interior. Barry removed the dome and the pulpit but left the building as presumably it was before, with galleries on all four sides. The west (liturgical east) gallery was removed in 1829 when the seating accommodation was enlarged. The chapel then seated 800 people.

Robert Anderson died on 22 March 1842. He had made the church fashionable, and both Manning and Pusey had preached for him there. A tablet with a bas-relief of his profile was erected to his memory in the chapel by the congregation. He left Trinity chapel to trustees. After the short curacy of the Rev. C. E. Kennaway the trustees presented to the chapel the Rev. Frederick William Robertson, who was the most important person in the history of this church and one of the most remarkable clergymen to appear on the Brighton scene throughout the nineteenth century.

Robertson was born on 3 February 1816. He was the eldest of the seven children of Captain Frederick Robertson of the Royal Artillery. He was educated at Beverley Grammar School and the Edinburgh Academy. He was at first very much drawn to the army but was articled by his father to a solicitor at Bury St Edmunds. He was not happy in this work and began instead to show an interest in the Church. As a result he was sent to Oxford and matriculated at Brasenose College in 1837. He read classics but did not take an honours degree. The Tractarian movement was then at its height in Oxford, but he never felt drawn towards it, having been brought up in the Evangelical tradition.

He was ordained on 12 July 1840 and took a curacy at Winchester. But after a year he had his first breakdown in health and had to go abroad. While in Switzerland he married Helen, daughter of Sir George William Denys, baronet, of Easton Neston, Northamptonshire, who was equerry to the Duke of Sussex. From 1842 to 1847 he was curate at Christ church, Cheltenham, but again relinquished the position through ill health and went abroad. On his return he was for two months in charge of the parish of St Ebbe's in Oxford, which was then the poorest quarter of the city. On receiving the offer of the Trinity chapel in Brighton he gave up St Ebbe's with some reluc-

15 The Rev. F. W. Robertson

tance but with the full understanding of the Bishop of Oxford, Dr Samuel Wilberforce.

He established himself at 9 Montpelier Terrace in Brighton and remained there until 1850, when he moved to 60 Montpelier Road. Both houses now have commemorative plaques on them. He very soon began to make an impact on life in Brighton. One of his aims was to interest what were then called the working class, and particularly young men, in Christianity. In 1848 he founded for their education the Working Men's Institute in Middle Street. After a short period there was a schism in this. The radical non-Christian members departed and the club was renamed the Mechanics' Institution. Robertson was also associated with the local branch of the Early Closing Association, which aimed at reducing the hours of work for shop assistants.

Robertson soon became noted for the nature of his sermons. He preached on the effect of religion on social, political, national and international life. For instance during the year of revolutions (1848), while not approving revolutionary methods, he welcomed the disappearance of the old authoritarian regimes. As as result he was sometimes accused of being a Democrat, as revolutionaries were then called, or a Socialist. But this was very far from the case. His biographer, Stopford A. Brooke, called him 'instinctively a Tory, by conviction a Liberal but never a Socialist'. In local politics he supported the Liberal party.

In church matters he was in favour of moderation. When the Roman Catholic Church embarked on the so-called papal aggression of 1850 Robertson considered this as no more than an error of judgment and urged moderation on the part of the Church of England. He was only a very moderate sabbatarian and refused to protest against the opening of the Great Exhibition of 1851 on Sundays. His great success within the Church in such a short period was truly remarkable in view of the fact that he belonged to no party within the Church. Although brought up as an Evangelical, he was never associated with that party in his work. Neither did he adhere to Tractarianism or to Christian Socialism. He hated to think of himself as a popular preacher. On 17 May 1853 he wrote to a friend: 'I cannot say how humiliated I feel at degenerating into the popular preacher of a fashionable watering-place' (*The Life and Letters of Frederick W. Robertson*, Stopford A. Brooke, 1860). Such of course he did become, as was demonstrated by the string of carriages which appeared each week at Trinity chapel. But he was very much more than this as well. He was in fact one of the first preachers to relate Christianity to life, and in so doing his sermons appealed to all sections of society.

With Robertson stress was never very far below the surface, and by 1852 he was already suffering from depression. This grew gradually worse. It was called overwork at the time but must have actually been a bad nervous breakdown. Early in 1853 his congregation offered to provide the money for him to employ a curate. He chose the Rev. Ernest Tower for this position. Unfortunately this choice was not acceptable to the vicar of Brighton, the Rev. H. M. Wagner, whom Tower had offended three years previously in the affairs of the Lewes Deanery of the Society for the Promotion of Christian Knowledge. Robertson, in his acutely nervous state, refused to select anyone else. So he never received any help. He grew worse, became partly paralysed and died on 15 August 1853, aged only 37. The cause of his death was at that time called 'brain fever'.

His funeral eight days later was a very grand affair. His tomb in the Extra Mural Cemetery, Brighton, takes the form of a low Egyptian pylon decorated with two bronze bas-relief medallions by Wyon depicting aspects of Robertson's ministry. One of these was given by his congregation and the other by the members of the Mechanics' Institution. Below the former is the inscription:

> Honoured as a Minister, Beloved as a Man, he awakened the
> holiest feelings in poor and rich, in ignorant and learned.
> Therefore he is lamented as their guide and comforter by many
> who, in the bond of brotherhood and in grateful remembrance,
> have erected this monument. Glory to the Saviour, who was his
> all.

A bust of Robertson was given to the town by Henry Willett and placed in the Royal Pavilion, later in the Town Hall. Another bust was placed in the Bodleian Library at Oxford. His portrait also exists, painted by C. J. Basebe. In 1861 a memorial window was inserted in the chapel of his own college, Brasenose College, Oxford. At his death an appeal was made to provide a testimonial to his work. This raised £1,100, of which £300 was given by Lady Byron who had been a friend of Robertson's for many years. The fund was used for the benefit of children. That his life and thought have had lasting value for other periods than his own is shown by the fact that his sermons, published posthumously, ran into twenty or more editions during the rest of the nineteenth century and were translated into many languages. Despite his independent status, perhaps even because of it, he still has a well-known place in the Church of England's history. As recently as 1926 a memorial to him was erected in Christ Church, Cheltenham, where he was curate for five years. But he is still generally called Robertson of Brighton. His appeal to bridge the gap between classes, parties and nations is still one which rings through the world and is insufficiently heard.

Robertson's successor at Trinity chapel was Dr John Griffith. He held the perpetual curacy from 1853 to 1856 and left to become principal or headmaster of Brighton College, which had been founded in 1847.

No alteration to Trinity chapel was made during Robertson's incumbency. Nor was any memorial to him erected in the church until fifteen years after his death. But in 1867 Duke Street was widened on the north side, and the Georgian house immediately adjoining the church was demolished. This provided an opportunity to enlarge the church. A chancel was added. This was at the west end, as the church, like so many in Brighton, is wrongly orientated. The west (liturgical east) window is a memorial to Robertson and illustrates subjects from his sermons.

In 1878 the Anderson family sold the freehold of the church for £6,500 to trustees for the Church of England. To this sum the family themselves contributed £1,000. By this date Amon Wilds's classical exterior was very much out of fashion. The trustees therefore employed Somers Clarke junior to modernise the church. He was the son of Somers Clarke who was clerk to the Brighton Vestry from 1830 to 1892. Trinity chapel was the first Brighton church which Somers Clarke altered and was his least good effort in church design. He gave the building a false Gothic east (liturgical west) front in flint, surmounted by an octagonal tower and with a single-storied porch projecting beyond it. The stuccoed classical south elevation, which was never meant to be seen, remained unaltered. The galleried interior with its clerestory of three-light windows was also left undisturbed, although galleries were out of fashion in the period 1885–7 when the adaptations were made.

In the twentieth century the church briefly returned to preaching fame during the incumbency of the Rev. Dr Reginald John Campbell. It was not the first time Campbell had ministered in Brighton, but his earlier period had been for another denomination. He went to Oxford with the intention of taking Anglican Orders, but at the last minute did not do so and joined the Congregational Church instead. His first cure, from 1893 to 1898 was that of Union Street chapel in Brighton. In 1898 this chapel was amalgamated with the Queen Square Congregational chapel under the name of Union church. He held this united ministry until 1903 and during this period attracted large congregations there by his outstanding sermons. In 1903 he received a call to the City Temple church in London, where he remained until 1915.

In 1916 he was ordained in the Church of England and after a short period at Birmingham cathedral became vicar of Christ church, Westminster, from 1917 to 1921. From 1924 to 1931 he was perpetual curate of Holy Trinity, Brighton, as Trinity chapel had by then come to be called. During this period the church regained to a certain extent the celebrity that it had enjoyed during Robertson's ministry, such that latecomers to services were not always sure of obtaining a seat. In 1930 Campbell became canon and chancellor of Chichester cathedral and retained these positions until his death a few years later.

Holy Trinity church was never allotted a separate parish, and as the centre

16 Holy Trinity church 1987

of the town became less and less residential the congregation dwindled somewhat. After the Second World War the diocesan authorities would have liked
to close the church. But owing to the rent derived from the Robertson Hall,
which adjoined the church on the north, the congregation was financially
independent. However, when the Rev. Paul James (1969–71) left to become
Dean of Quebec in Canada no new perpetual curate was appointed, and the
services were henceforward conducted on an *ad hoc* basis. At the end of
December 1984 the church was finally closed, and the congregation now
has services of its own at the Chapel Royal nearby. The building of Holy
Trinity church is likely to be taken over by the Brighton Museum and converted into a special museum of Brighton's own history.

6

ST MARY'S CHURCH

The fourth proprietory chapel to be built in Brighton during the 1820s was St Mary's church, Rock Gardens. The erection of this building was partly due to the Lord Lieutenant of Sussex, the third Earl of Egremont, of Petworth House. He then had a house in Brighton on the east side of Upper Rock Gardens. This was probably built in about 1800 and was an L-shaped stuccoed mansion. The main elevation faced south and had eleven windows with two curved bays of two storeys with pediments over. The entrance was in the west front of five bays with a rectangular porch. Lord Egremont died in 1837, and his successors did not continue to live in the house. It was demolished later in the century, when the houses on the east side of Upper Rock Gardens were built. Except that the street to the north bears the name of Egremont Place the house is now largely forgotten. But a drawing of it by W. A. Delamotte is in the Brighton Art Gallery. In the present St Mary's church there is also a large watercolour of the first St Mary's which clearly shows Lord Egremont's house to the north.

When Barnard Gregory built St Margaret's church, Cannon Place, he had some thought of erecting another proprietory chapel in St James's Street. The private Act of Parliament dated 10 June 1825 which provided for the building of St Margaret's also empowered Gregory to build another church in St James's Street. The terms of the Act were similar to those relating to Trinity chapel in that Gregory was empowered to appoint a perpetual curate for a term of forty years, who was to receive a stipend of £150 a year out of special pew rents. But Gregory never carried out the idea of building a second church and in 1826 sold the proprietory rights to Charles Elliott of Grove House, Clapham, and Westfield Lodge, Brighton. Lord Egremont then gave a piece of land immediately adjoining his garden on the south on which to build the church.

Charles Elliott was an interesting man and the founder of a family who were important in church life in Brighton during the next forty years. He had been a partner in the firm of Davis & Elliott, later Elliott & Co. of 97 (now 104) New Bond Street, London. This was then the chief rival to Waring & Gillow as the best furniture suppliers in London. Amongst their patrons were George III and George IV. The firm was one of the first importers of French furniture into England. They supplied nearly £2,000's worth of furniture to George IV as Prince of Wales for the first Royal Pavilion. Charles Elliott moved to Brighton soon after 1800 and lived at Westfield Lodge on the West Cliff, as that part of King's Road was then called. He was a Town Commissioner from 1809 to 1827. He was a pious man and one of the founders of the Church Missionary Society. He was the brother-in-law of John Venn, rector of Clapham, who was the central figure of the Clapham sect. This numbered amongst its members such a well-known figure as William Wilberforce. Charles Elliott was also a member. He died in 1832, aged 81, and is buried in the church-yard of the old parish church of St Andrew's, Hove, in a table-tomb immediately adjoining the south wall of the church. A commemorative tablet was also erected in St Mary's church. But when the church was rebuilt later in the century this and all the other Elliott memorials were banished to the north-west vestry of the new building, where they are hardly seen at all.

Three of Charles Elliott's children who are buried at Hove in the same grave with him had ecclesiastical connections. His daughter Charlotte wrote hymns, of which the best known are 'Nearer my God to thee' and 'Just as I am without one plea'. Two of his sons (Henry Venn and Edward Bishop Elliott) took Holy Orders. It was in fact for the benefit of Henry Venn Elliott that his father built St Mary's church.

For an architect Elliott turned to Amon Henry Wilds, the son of Amon Wilds who, with Charles Augustus Busby, was building Kemp Town and Brunswick Town, Hove at the time. Classical architecture then reigned supreme in the realm of proprietory chapels. So for the church Wilds chose to reproduce a Greek temple, the temple of Nemesis at Athens. The building was orientated north to south. It was entered on the south side through a portico of four fluted Doric columns with a triglyph frieze and a pediment over. The south elevation was not unlike the Unitarian chapel in New Road, which A. M. Wilds had built six years before. The west (liturgical north) front had six giant sash windows of many panes. The contract to build the

17 The original St Mary's church. Drawing by W. A. Delamotte

church was for £2,000. But Henry Venn Elliott afterwards claimed that the
building had cost his father £10,000 on account of the bankruptcy of the
builder, the carelessness of his lawyer and the roguery of the vendor (Barnard
Gregory).

The interior had galleries on three sides resting on fluted columns. There
was a shallow chancel flanked by pilasters. The altar was surmounted by
a picture of the Cross and flanked by pulpits on shaped bases with elegant
curved staircases. There were box-pews throughout. At the north (liturgical
east) end of the galleries were two special pews, one of which was probably
the pew that had been set aside for Lord Egremont under the arrangement
with him. There were 240 free sittings for the poor and accommodation
for 947 people in all.

The church was consecrated by the Bishop of Chichester, Dr R. J. Carr,
on 18 January 1827. As part of the understanding with Lord Egremont, the
first perpetual curate was to have been Dr Edward Everard, who was then

18 The interior of the original St Mary's church. Drawing by W. A. Delamotte

one of the curates at the parish church. But after a long and complicated negotiation between Everard, Barnard Gregory and the new vicar of Brighton, the Rev. H. M. Wagner, Everard became instead the first perpetual curate of St Margaret's church. This left Charles Elliott free to appoint to the perpetual curacy of St Mary's his son, for whose benefit he had in fact acquired the freehold of the building. This freehold also devolved on Henry Venn Elliott when his father died in 1832.

The Rev. Henry Venn Elliott was born on 17 January 1792. He was the eldest of Charles Elliott's children by his second marriage to Eling, daughter of the Rev. Henry Venn of Queen's College, Cambridge and vicar of Huddersfield and later of Yelling in Huntingdonshire. He was educated at Trinity College, Cambridge, where he read mathematics. Although the subject is said not to have interested him, he passed out as fourteenth wrangler. In 1816 he was elected a fellow of the College. He then embarked on the grand tour. He remained abroad for three years and penetrated as far as Turkey.

19 The Rev. H. V. Elliott

From his earliest years he was determined to enter the Church. He was ordained deacon in 1823 and priest the following year. For two years he had charge of the parish of Ampton in Suffolk. But in August 1826 he entered into possession of the new St Mary's church at Brighton almost before the building was completed.

In 1833 Henry Venn Elliot married Julia Anne, daughter of John Marshall of Hallsteads, Ulleswater. His first married home was at 33 Brunswick Terrace, Hove, but in 1835 he moved to 31 Brunswick Square, where he remained until his death. He ministered at St Mary's church for nearly forty years. During this period he was the leader in Brighton of the Evangelical party within the Church of England. As such he was a resolute champion of sabbatarianism, the principal opponent of the so-called papal aggression of 1850 and an equal foe of the ritualist or Tractarian movement within the Church of England. Like his father, he was a great supporter of the Church Missionary Society. But his chief work in Brighton, apart from St Mary's church, was the foundation of St Mary's Hall school for the daughters of clergy. The first Marquess of Bristol gave the land for this, and the foundation stone of the building was laid by his daughter, Lady Augusta Seymour, on 21 April 1834. The Tudor-Gothic building was designed in an honorary capacity by George Basevi, whose parents were neighbours of Elliott's in Brunswick Square. It cost £4,250. When the school was opened in August 1836 there was accommodation for a lady superintendent, five governesses and a hundred pupils. They were looked after by a staff of a housekeeper, six maids and a gardener. Elliott himself gave at least £2,250 towards the cost of the building and 1,000 books out of his library.

Ideas have so changed since Elliott's time that it is difficult to assess the nature and quality of St Mary's Hall in its early days. Elliott was a friend of the Rev. William Carus Wilson of Castleton Hall, Lancashire, who had founded a Clergy Daughters' School at Cowan Bridge in that county. Charlotte Brontë and her four sisters attended this school. Two of them died of consumption during the period of their attendance. Charlotte Brontë described or pilloried, as the case may be, the school in *Jane Eyre*. Even if one allows for her extreme sensitivity and her brilliant imagination as a novelist, it is difficult to escape the conclusion that the Cowan Bridge school was a grim establishment which could almost be described as an institution for breaking the spirits of potential governesses. As St Mary's Hall was deliberately modelled on this school one wonders how much the atmosphere of St Mary's Hall was dominated by the same heartless spirit, in which life was considered only as a vale of tears and all tribulations were to be welcomed as the will of God.

Elliott played a major part in the building of St Mark's Church, principally to act as the chapel for St Mary's Hall. He gave £1,500 towards the cost of the church. This was consecrated on 21 September 1849. Lord Bristol, who gave the land for the building of the church, wanted Elliott to transfer his ministry from St Mary's to St Mark's, but Elliott refused to make the change. In December 1860 he attended the former Prime Minister, Lord Aberdeen, on his death-bed. Elliott himself died on 24 January 1865, aged 83. He was buried in his father's grave in the church-yard of the old parish church at Hove. A tablet in his memory was also erected at St Mary's church. At the rebuilding of the church this was repositioned in the north-west vestry.

He was succeeded at St Mary's by his youngest son, the Rev. Julius Marshall Elliott. The latter was born in 1841 and was educated at Brighton College and Trinity College, Cambridge. He was ordained deacon in 1865 and became a curate at Pluckley in Kent. When his father died he was only 28 and had not been ordained priest. H. V. Elliott's brother-in-law, Canon John Babington, therefore acted as locum tenens for him for a year until he had been fully ordained. He only held the living for four years. He was an early alpinist and was the first man to scale the north face of the Matterhorn. He was killed on 27 July 1869 as the result of a climbing accident on the Schreck-horn in Switzerland and was buried at Grindelwald. A tablet to his memory is also to be found in the north-west vestry of St Mary's church.

The original forty-year period having elapsed, further presentations rested with the vicar of Brighton. Henry Wagner appointed the Rev. W. W. God-den, who only served for four years. In 1855 St Mary's had been allotted a district of 3,000 inhabitants. But when in 1873 the whole parish of Brighton was reorganised this district was reallotted to St James's church and a new and larger parish given to St Mary's. Julius Elliott's nephew, C. A. Elliott, made a gift of the freehold of the building and the pew rents to the Ecclesiastical Commissioners. They abolished the pew rents and made over the advowson to trustees. At the same time the Rev. Arthur Thornhill Waugh became incumbent as the first vicar.

The church was then in a very poor state of repair after nearly fifty years' existence. So it was proposed to spend £2,500 on its restoration, towards which the Elliott family promised £1,000. But on 16 June 1876 part of the

20 St Mary's church 1943

walls and roof collapsed. One cannot help feeling that this calamity must
have been welcome to many people, as in 1876 the reproduction of a pagan
temple was the worst kind of image for a Christian church. The parish
decided to start afresh and build a new church – naturally a Gothic one –
at an estimated cost of £12,000. For the architect they chose William Emer-
son, who was then aged 33. He eventually became president of the Royal
Institute of British Architects (1899–1902) and was knighted in 1902. But,
like Sir Arthur Blomfield, he was more highly esteemed in his own lifetime
than since. His best works were in India.

The foundation stone of the new church was laid by Blanche Elliott, one
of Henry Venn Elliott's daughters, on 29 May 1877. Building took two years,
and during that time services for the congregation were held in the music
room of the Royal Pavilion, of all unecclesiastical places. The eventual cost
amounted to £15,231. The church was reconsecrated on 15 October 1878

21 The interior of St Mary's church 1987

by the Bishop of Chichester, Dr Richard Durnford. The new building was a complete contrast to the old. It was of red brick in a style which Pevsner called Early English but is really French Gothic. Owing to the constriction of the site only the west and south elevations can be seen. The whole badly needs the tower which should have stood at the south-west corner and – judging by the design – would have been a magnificent affair. But this was never built. The interior is much more impressive. The entrance on the south (liturgical west) is via a baptistry raised four steps above the level of the rest of the church. This gives a splendid view of the nave and aisles with their stone arcades. The five-sided apsidal chancel is flanked by chapels, used as vestries. Behind these is an ingeniously contrived narrow ambulatory. There is a stone reredos with a carved panel above the altar. The matching pulpit is built round a piece of granite from the Schreckhorn in memory of Julius Marshall Elliott. The baptistry has a round alabaster font with carved wooden canopy.

In 1948 St James's church was closed, and its parish, which had once formed part of St Mary's parish, was reunited to it. When St James's church was demolished in about 1975 two memorials from that church were moved to the north aisle of St Mary's. These commemorate the Rev. C. D. Maitland, who had been the perpetual curate of St James's from 1828 to 1865, and the Rev. John Purchas, who was his successor (1865–72) and whose introduction of ritualist services there caused great local and even national disturbance. (For further details of this controversy see *The Wagners of Brighton* by Anthony Wagner and Antony Dale, 1983.) Also from St James's church is the plate comprising a silver-gilt paten and chalice, given to the older church in 1820 by Nathaniel Kemp of Ovingdean Hall, father of the stained-glass artist, Charles Eamer Kempe.

7

ST ANDREW'S CHURCH
Waterloo Street, Hove

St Andrew's church, Waterloo Street, Hove, was exactly contemporary with St Margaret's church, Cannon Place, Brighton, and the three churches that have just been described.

By 1820 the houses along the West Cliff in Brighton had reached the western boundary of the parish. When Brunswick Town was built it therefore had to be sited in the adjoining parish of Hove. The land which formed the site was known as Wick Farm and belonged to the Rev. Thomas Scutt, although he no longer lived at the farmhouse. Brunswick Town was built between 1825 and 1828. The architects were Amon Wilds and Charles Augustus Busby. Like Kemp Town the estate was intended to be a complete town on its own. It therefore needed a place of worship. Strangely enough neither the owner nor the architects of the estate provided this, despite the fact that the proprietor was a clergyman. This was actually done by another clergyman who played a prominent part in the church affairs of Brighton at this period, Dr Edward Everard. Prior to 1824 he had been one of the curates at Brighton parish church and, as the vicar, Dr R. J. Carr, was also Dean of Hereford, Everard had lived at the Brighton vicarage. When H. M. Wagner arrived in Brighton, as was mentioned in the preceding chapter, it was at first intended that Everard should be the first perpetual curate of St Mary's church. But this never came about, and Everard became instead the first perpetual curate of St Margaret's. He moved to a house in Cannon Place near that church. In 1825 he was also presented to the rectory of South-wick, Sussex and held both incumbencies in plurality until 1828.

Everard owned land in what became Waterloo Street, Hove. He obtained permission from the vicar of Hove, the Rev. James Skanier Clarke, and the patron of the living, the Rev. Henry Plimley, prebendary of the Prebend

22 The original interior of St Andrew's church, Waterloo Street, Hove

of Hove Ecclesia, to build St Andrew's church on his land in Waterloo Street for the benefit of Brunswick Town. Excavation of the site began in April 1827. The work took just over a year. For his architect Everard turned to Charles Barry, who was a friend of his. Barry was already working in Brighton at St Peter's church and at the Sussex County Hospital, of which Everard was one of the joint honorary secretaries. Barry, who was freshly returned from his grand tour, designed the west end of the church, which is really all the exterior that can be seen, in the Italianate style. This was the first instance in which this style was used in England. Barry used it again in Brighton about two years later when he came to design for Thomas Attree the villa in Queen's Park which was later known as the Xaverian College.

The interior of St Andrew's was that of a typical Regency preaching-house, except that there was only one gallery, at the west end of the church. There was no chancel, and the altar-piece comprised three round-headed niches containing the Ten Commandments, the Lord's Prayer and the Creed. These were flanked by the usual pair of pulpits but this time without prominent curved staircases to them. There were box-pews throughout and burial vaults below the church. On the north side of the building was a narrow schoolroom fitted with desks. This was later converted into a vestry.

67

Everard obtained a private Act of Parliament similar to those governing Trinity chapel and St Mary's church. He or his successors in title were empowered to appoint a perpetual curate for the initial period of forty years, after which time the right of presentation passed to the vicar of Hove. This Act was dated 3 April 1828. Only eighty free seats were provided, but sufficient pews were set aside to produce the usual income of £150 a year for the stipend of the perpetual curate. The church was consecrated by the Bishop of Chichester, Dr R. J. Carr, on 5 July 1828. It rapidly became very fashionable, and because of the social success of Brunswick Town as a place of residence soon had the most aristocratic congregation of any church in Brighton or Hove.

Everard presented himself to the living and in 1829 moved from Cannon Place into Wick House, where he ran an academy for young gentlemen. When William IV came to the throne the King appointed Everard as chaplain to his household, and Everard officiated at services in the Royal Chapel whenever the Court was in residence in the Royal Pavilion. In 1833 the King inspected Everard's school at Wick House. When the Pluralities Act was passed in 1838 Everard, being also rector of Southwick, was obliged to give up the perpetual curacy of St Andrew's and was succeeded by the Rev. Owen Marden (1838–56). At the same time he moved from Wick House to 24 Brunswick Square. He died in the following year.

By 1882 the liturgical arrangements of St Andrew's church were no longer in accord with the ecclesiastical ideas of the time. In order to erect a chancel the perpetual curate and proprietor, the Rev. Daniel Winham (1868–94) therefore purchased at the cost of £2,000 the stable buildings which immediately adjoined the church on the east. Sir Charles Barry had died in 1860. Therefore Winham commissioned Barry's son, Edward Middleton Barry, the architect of Covent Garden Theatre in London, to design the addition to St Andrew's. E. M. Barry fortunately decided to keep within the classical idiom. He designed a tripartite chancel with an apsidal-ended sanctuary flanked by recesses with round windows. The sanctuary is set behind Ionic columns and is panelled with nine round-headed arches. Over it is a dome painted with gold stars on a blue background and lit by a lunette window. There was space in the addition to the north-west of the sanctuary for a new organ. In 1889 this was given an elaborate case in memory of Thomas William Wing.

In addition to the price of acquiring the site the construction of the chancel

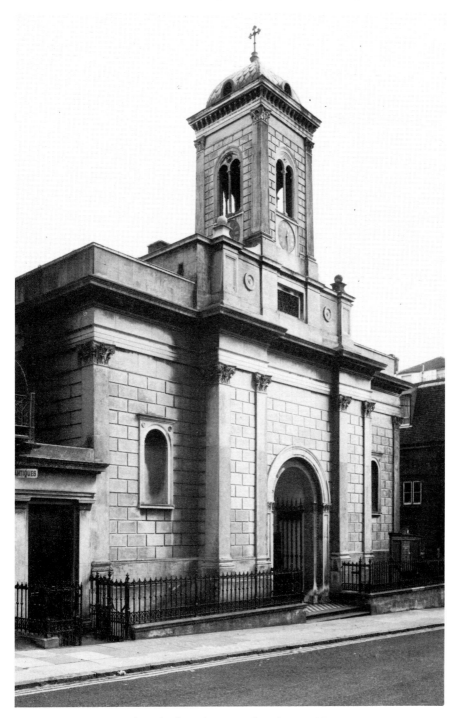

23 St Andrew's church, Waterloo Street, Hove 1987

cost £5,203. 10s. Of this, £2,875 was raised by public subscription. The balance was provided by the proprietor and perpetual curate, Daniel Winham. His successor, the Rev. C. A. Moull (1894–1906) was the first perpetual curate of the church to be appointed by the vicar of Hove.

St Andrew's was not again altered until the Rev. Stanley E. Kirkley came to the church in 1924. He was perpetual curate for twenty-nine years. In 1925 he commissioned W. H. Randoll Blacking to design several embellishments which would transform the church into 'a little bit of Italy' to match the exterior. The most important of these was a baldacchino over the altar of fluted columns with foliated capitals surmounted by figures of angels and with a pediment facing the nave. At the west end under the gallery he inserted a new marble font also surmounted by a similar but smaller baldacchino. A new pulpit and altar-rails were provided. The existing stained-glass windows made the church rather dark, so these were mostly replaced. Less happily, most of the memorial tablets were banished to the narthex at the west end of the church. But four of rather greater size and interest survive in their original positions. These commemorate the following: General Lord Fitzroy Somerset, Governor of the Cape of Good Hope, who died in 1831; Sir George Dallas, baronet, of the Indian Civil Service, who died in 1833 (sculptor, Ternouth); Lord George Seymour, the youngest brother of Thackeray's Marquess of Steine, who died in 1848; and Charles Brownlow, second Baron Lurgan, who died in 1882. The cost of these alterations in 1925 was £4,000, which was contributed by the congregation.

In recent years the congregation of St Andrew's had dwindled somewhat. It was therefore amalgamated with the parish of All Saints in the Drive but is now united with the parish of St Patrick's in Cambridge Road.

8

ST ANDREW'S CHURCH, CHURCH ROAD, HOVE

(Hove old parish church)

The original village of Hove comprised a single street lying along the line of what is now Hove Street. The manor house, which was built by the Tredcroft family in the eighteenth century, stood at the north-east end of the street. This was unfortunately and most unnecessarily demolished in 1936 and is the greatest architectural loss that either Brighton or Hove has suffered during the last fifty years. The only building outside the line of the street was the parish church, which lay about a quarter of a mile to the north-east in the fields. The only access to the church was from the west. There was no road on the Brighton side.

The first building on the site was Saxon. This was replaced by a transitional-Norman nave with aisles and a west tower. The chancel was added or rebuilt in the thirteenth century. As the centuries progressed the church gradually fell into ruins. No certain explanation of this can be given. It has been suggested that the church was sacked in a raid by the French, or that a fire occurred in the sixteenth century. It seems more likely that, after much of the village had been overrun by the sea, the remaining inhabitants were just unable to maintain the building. As late as 1801 the total number of inhabitants was only 101 and in 1811 only 312. In 1531 the parish of Hove was united with the much larger and more important parish of Preston to the north-east. By 1724 the church was reduced to the five bays of the nave with the tower partly in ruins. The chancel had almost gone. Soon afterwards the aisles were unroofed and the arches of the arcades blocked. Services were only held once in six weeks. In 1801 the tower finally collapsed, and with it went the westernmost bay of the nave. The stones of the tower were removed to the park of Goodwood House to build a 'Gothick' ruin or folly. To accommodate the two bells from the tower a

71

small wooden bellcote was added at the east end of the remaining building.

From this parlous state the church was rescued by the construction of Brunswick Town in the years following 1824 and by the arrival of a new vicar of Hove-cum-Preston in 1834. The expansion of Brighton westwards having reached the parish boundary, this new town was built within the parish of Hove. Municipal government for it was provided by the passing of the Brunswick Square Act of 1830. Its spiritual needs were met by the erection of St Andrew's church, Waterloo Street. But it was obvious that the town would spread further west in due course. The new incumbent, the Rev. Walter Kelly, had no doubt that an enlarged and improved parish church was needed or very soon would be. The result was the holding of a Vestry meeting on 14 September 1833 in the Kerrison Arms Inn, Brunswick Street East, to consider the question of restoring or rebuilding the parish church. At an adjourned meeting on 20 September an amendment was moved to the effect that, as the old church stood on a remote site, a committee should be appointed to consider another site for a new church. This amendment was negatived, and it was decided to rebuild the old church.

A week later (28 September) the Vestry resolved to ask George Basevi to survey the building and report on it. His choice as architect was no doubt due to the fact that his parents were resident at 37 Brunswick Square. His father, George Basevi senior, was chairman of the Brighton magistrates from 1838 to 1843 and also a deputy lieutenant of Sussex. The latter's sister, Maria, had married Isaac D'Israeli and was the mother of Benjamin Disraeli, Lord Beaconsfield. George Basevi junior acted as the honorary architect of St Mary's Hall, Brighton in 1834 but is better known as the architect of Belgrave Square, London, and of the Fitzwilliam Museum in Cambridge.

In early December Basevi reported that rebuilding the parish church to its former dimensions would cost £1,870 plus £56. 7s. for the fittings. On 15 February 1834 the Vestry resolved to seek the permission of the Ecclesiastical Commissioners to borrow £2,000 from Samuel Preston Child of Clapton on the security of the rates, repayable over twenty years. A church rate of two and a half pence in the pound was levied as a first step towards meeting the liability. George Basevi's fee of £56. 7s. was paid by his father. The lay rector of the church, William Stanford of Preston manor, declined to accept responsibility for rebuilding the chancel.

The work of rebuilding was entrusted to Butler & Son of Paddington Green. Their estimate amounted to £1,920, plus £194 for extra masonry.

24 St Andrew's church, Church Road, Hove (the old parish church)

In 1834 the Gothic revival was still at an early stage. The Early English and Decorated styles had not yet acquired a stranglehold on taste as being the only styles admissible. Just as Barry, in 1824, had felt free to design St Peter's church, Brighton, in Perpendicular style, so Basevi was able to use Norman for his rebuilding of St Andrew's, no doubt on the grounds that the existing pillars of the nave arcades were of that period. In fact according to the ideas of the time he probably looked upon the rebuilding of the church as a restoration and, with that in mind, gave the chancel pointed lancet windows because the medieval chancel had been a thirteenth-century addition in Early English style. In fact his work was not a restoration, as the whole of the exterior dates from 1834 to 1836. Neo-Norman is an unusual style. The only other example in Sussex is Falmer church. It is also a harsh style which seems not to age with the years or to lose its rather unyielding characteristics. St Andrew's externally is somewhat of this nature.

The interior is surprisingly different, for here enough medieval work survives to give the building a comfortable, even cosy, atmosphere. The round Norman columns and the pointed arches of the nave arcades are the dominant feature. Their effect is enhanced by the survival of the original tie-beams and braced crown-posts of the roof in all but the westernmost bay.

The work of rebuilding took just over two years. The church was reopened for worship on 18 June 1836. It contained 430 seats, of which 350 were free. The church was soon filled by the rising population of Hove, and in 1839 a west gallery with a Gothic frontage was inserted to accommodate 200 more people. The north-east vestry was added in 1841 at the cost of £134 and was designed in Early English style to match the chancel. In 1842 the church was first heated with hot-water pipes.

Of the post-medieval features in the church, the most important comprises the wall-tablets. They all date from after 1836 but contribute greatly to the atmosphere of the building. They form the best series of memorials in any Brighton or Hove church. The chancel contains only one memorial – a late one commemorating the Rev. Walter Kelly, who was the last incumbent of the joint benefice of Hove-cum-Preston. He was responsible for the rebuilding of the church from 1834 to 1836 and held the living for forty-four years. He resigned in 1878 and died nine years later, aged 85. He was buried in a table-tomb to the east of the church, which had been erected for his father, Patrick Kelly, LLD, of Finsbury Square, London, who died in Brighton in 1842, aged 87.

The most elegant memorial in the church is over the side-altar on the east wall of the south aisle. This commemorates Elizabeth, wife of Thomas Yard, who died on 14 February 1836. A bas-relief medallion shows an angel wafting her soul to heaven. To the south of the chancel arch is the vault of the Vallance family, who were lords of the manor of Hove for more than 150 years and occupied Hove manor house. At the east end of the south aisle are tablets to three generations of John Vallance, who died in 1812, 1833 and 1851 respectively.

In the south aisle is also the memorial of the most famous man to be buried at St Andrew's, the watercolour painter, Antony Vandyke Copley Fielding. He lived for some years at 2 Lansdowne Place, Hove, but died in Worthing in 1855. He is buried in a table-tomb in the north-east corner of the church-yard, which had been erected during his lifetime for some of his children.

On his memorial in the south aisle are these lines composed by the Rev. C. Townsend:

> Fielding, by common fate tho' doomed to die,
> Thou leav'st to us a deathless legacy.
> Through thee did Nature open and dispense
> Her hidden charm of simplest elegance.
> The living Waves that o'er the Ocean flow
> Scattering their sparkling freshness as they go,
> The space aerial and the tender line
> And willing beauty of the Downs were thine.
> Their breathing souls to thee in charge were given.
> Then gav'st them us – thyself in heaven.

To the east of the Copley Fielding monument in the church is a tablet to a well-known Brighton solicitor, John Sidney McWhinnie, who died at Nice – then part of the kingdom of Sardinia – on 13 December 1857. He had been a partner in the firm of Attree, Cooper & McWhinnie of 8 Ship Street, which later became Howlett & Clarke and is the oldest firm of solicitors in Brighton.

To the north of the chancel arch is an interesting and unusual tablet to the memory of an Italian named Joseph Pecchio, who died in 1835, aged 49. The inscription, in Latin, composed by his wife, calls him a chevallier from Milan who was a political exile from his country. 'May England, the land of the free, ever remain a refuge for the political and religious exile.'

In front of this memorial is the vault of the Basevi family. But they also have a memorial in the north-west corner of the north aisle which was sculpted by the Brighton sculptor, William Pepper. This commemorates George Basevi senior, who died on 25 February 1853, aged 79, his wife, Bathsheba, and his daughter, Emma. His son, George Basevi junior, the architect of St Andrew's church, is buried in the precincts of Ely cathedral, where he met his death in 1845, aged only 51, by falling from one of the west towers – perhaps the only architect to suffer such a fate since William of Sens in Canterbury cathedral in 1179.

Near to the Basevi wall-tablet is a memorial to another of Brighton and Hove's well-to-do clergymen: the Rev. Thomas Richard Rooper of Wick Hall. He had been rector of Abbots Ripton in Huntingdonshire, then from 1856 to 1863 the perpetual curate and probably also the proprietor of St

Andrew's church, Waterloo Street, Hove. He died on 7 April 1865. Adjoining his memorial on the west is a more elaborate tablet decorated with military emblems to Thomas Richard Rooper's son, Major Edward Rooper of the Rifle Brigade, who died at sea of a wound incurred at the Battle of Inkerman in 1854.

The only other memorial in the north aisle that is of interest is that of Lieutenant Henry Sanderson, who died on 2 October 1852, aged 23. He was the resident engineer and private secretary of the governor of the island of St Lucia. The memorial shows a bas-relief of his profile, mourned by three female figures.

Some of the tombs in the church-yard, in addition to those that have already been mentioned, are of interest. To the south of the chancel is the table-tomb of the Elliott family. Charles Elliott of Westfield Lodge, Brighton, who started the furniture firm of Elliott & Co., died in 1832 and is buried here. Amongst the numerous members of his family who share the grave with him are his two sons, the Rev. Henry Venn Elliott, the first perpetual curate of St Mary's church, Brighton, and the founder of St Mary's Hall (died 1865), and the Rev. Edward Bishop Elliott, the second perpetual curate of St Mark's church, Brighton (died 1875), and Charles Elliott's daughter, Charlotte, the hymn writer, who died in 1871.

To the south of this grave is the granite cross which commemorates the Rev. Dr James O'Brien, the first perpetual curate of St Patrick's church, Hove, who died in 1884. Near this grave is the headstone of Sir George Everest, who was Surveyor General of India from 1832 till 1843. He was largely responsible for the great trigonometrical survey of India which was carried out between 1817 and 1841. In this the exact height of the highest mountain in the world was first recorded and was given the English name of Mount Everest after him, although the mountain already had a Tibetan name. Sir George Everest died in 1866 but seems not to have been a resident in either Brighton or Hove.

To the north-west of the church is the tomb of Admiral Sir George Augustus Westphal, RN. This has rather incongruously been made into the pivot of a turning place for vehicles approaching the church, but at least its original position has been respected. Westphal was born in 1785 and was present at the Battle of Trafalgar as a midshipman on board HMS *Victory*. During the battle he was wounded in the head. When he was carried down to the lower deck Nelson was already there dying but recognised him and said, 'What, poor fellow, are you here too?' Nelson's coat was hurriedly rolled up and placed under Westphal's head as a pillow. His wound bled profusely, and some of his hair became so encrusted with one of the epaulettes of the coat that it could only be separated from the coat by cutting off two of the bullions from the epaulette. These Westphal treasured all his life. Many years later when Nelson's coat was acquired for the nation Westphal was consulted as to whether it was in fact the coat that Nelson was wearing when he was mortally wounded. He was able to confirm its genuineness by pointing out the space of the two missing bullions. The coat is now in the National Maritime Museum at Greenwich, and this space can clearly be seen. Westphal had a distinguished career in the Navy and went through every commissioned rank up to that of full admiral. In retirement he lived for nearly forty years at 2 Brunswick Square and was a Brighton magistrate. He died at his house on 12 January 1875, aged 90.

On Walter Kelly's retirement in 1878 the church and parish underwent considerable changes. The two parishes of Hove and Preston were separated by Order in Council, and when the Rev. Thomas, afterwards Canon, Peacey was appointed vicar in 1879 it was of Hove only. The vicarage, which Walter Kelly had built, was in Preston. Therefore Thomas Peacey's first priority was to build a vicarage for Hove. But this belongs to the story of All Saints church. From the first, Peacey intended to build a new parish church, but this had to wait for ten years. Meanwhile the interior of St Andrew's was restored. The work was entrusted to the builder, J. T. Chappell and cost £920. 7s. 7d. It probably included the removal of the box-pews which had survived from the old unrestored church. If these included a three-decker pulpit, this was replaced by the simple Gothic version of today. The font in the tower is slightly earlier as it was erected in 1865 in memory of Henry Crawford. According to the wording of Walter Kelly's memorial, the chancel was 'adorned' in his memory. By this is probably meant that the east wall was decorated with mosaics as a sort of reredos in the place of the panels of the Commandments, the Creed and the Lord's Prayer which had been put up in 1851.

At the same time (1880) the church-yard suffered its first curtailment. The old church had been surrounded by a fairly large grave-yard. But as early as twenty years after the rebuilding of the church it was clear that further spaces for graves would be needed. Therefore in 1858 the parish acquired a large piece of land to the north for the purpose. This was very extensive, as it went right back to what is now Malvern Street. This cost £1,600. In 1880 secular interference raised its ugly head for the first time. Thirty-one feet along the south front of the church-yard was compulsorily acquired by Act of Parliament for the widening or making of Church Road. Historically this was a very destructive measure as this part of the church-yard contained most of the older and historic graves. It was also a most unfortunate precedent for the use of an irresistible force like an Act of Parliament. The bodies interred on the land were removed to Hove cemetery. Amongst the tombs which were then destroyed must have been that of Charles Augustus Busby, who died on 18 September 1834. Its removal was a great historical loss. He was one of the architects of Kemp Town, Brighton and Brunswick Town, Hove. His co-architect and partner, Amon Wilds senior, was buried in St Nicholas's church-yard, Brighton, in the previous year, but fortunately his tomb was respected when that church-yard was relandscaped after the Second World War.

With the building of All Saints church in the Drive, St Andrew's ceased to be the parish church of Hove and from 1892 was a chapel of ease for sixty-five years. It was given a conventional district in 1942. But this did not give the parish the independence that it wanted. So after raising enough money to provide an endowment of £300 a year and build a vicarage, St Andrew's was given its own parish by Order in Council in 1957.

Four years earlier the lych-gate in the centre of the south wall of the church-yard had been erected to the design of W. Earle Yates. This was the gift of the Brighton Shiverers Swimming Club in memory of those of its members who were killed in the two world wars.

In 1972–3 the church-yard suffered its second amputation by Act of Parliament. The whole of the northern half, which had been closed for burials since 1882, was conveyed to the County Council to provide land for a new school to replace St Andrew's school in George Street, which had been built in 1858. This involved the loss of a very attractive green lung for that part of Hove. Of the graves removed in the operation the only one claimed by living relatives comprised the family vault of Lord Lurgan (1831–82). This was removed to Hove cemetery at the cost of £1,500. Probably the most interesting man whose grave was destroyed at this time was the Rev. Joseph Sortain. He died on 23 July 1866. He had been minister of the Countess of Huntingdon's church in North Street, Brighton, for twenty-nine years and played a leading part in the church life of that period. When the new school was built the land was divided off by a most inelegant fence, topped with barbed-wire like a prison. No attempt has been made to blot this out with a merciful hedge. Between this fence and the church a badly designed 'garden of remembrance' has been laid out for the disposal of cremated remains. This has no element of a garden about it at all. The result of these unfortunate developments is that the north part of the church-yard now presents a most unattractive spectacle.

More destructive historically has been the building of a parish hall on the south-east corner of the church-yard. Here the graves were older in date and therefore of greater historical interest. But no attempt was made to save or move to another site those that were of aesthetic or historic distinction. Amongst those destroyed was a very fine table-tomb of Sir David Scott, baronet, of Sillwood House, Sillwood Place, Brighton. He had been a director of the East India Company from 1814 to 1819. When he came to live in Brighton he played a prominent part in local affairs and was chairman of the Brighton magistrates for many years. He died in London on 18 June 1858. His wife, Caroline, Lady Scott, who lived at 22 Brunswick Terrace after his death, was buried in the same grave in 1870.

9

ST JOHN THE EVANGELIST'S CHURCH

St Margaret's and the four churches that were contemporary with it were all built for the benefit of fashionable residents and visitors. They did contain some free seats but very few. The poor of Brighton were largely dependent on the parish church and to some extent on the new St Peter's. By 1830 the population of Brighton was about 40,000. Of these, it was reckoned that about 18,000 were people who could be called poor or at least were not able to afford pew rents. Yet there were only 3,000 free sittings in the existing churches. Consequently when Henry Wagner became vicar of Brighton in 1824 he made it his first priority to provide a series of new churches in the poorer districts of the town in which the majority of the seats would be free.

The first of these churches was All Souls, Eastern Road. This area was then and remained throughout the nineteenth century one of the poorest districts in Brighton. The church was built between July 1833 and April 1834 and designed by Messrs Mew, builders who also built Wagner's new vicarage in Montpelier Road. The church was a very simple stuccoed classical building. Only the north elevation was exposed, and the chief feature was a low tower, which was a later addition at the west end, with a clock-face. The interior had galleries on three sides with Gothic detail, box-pews and a central three-decker pulpit. The church was built most inexpensively for £3,082. 10s. 8d., of which the Society for the Building and Enlargement of Churches gave £500. The remainder was raised by public subscription. The vicar himself contributed £150. Nine hundred and sixty of the 1,300 seats were free. It was the first church in Brighton to have a surpliced choir. The church was remodelled and a chancel added by Edmund Scott and his partner, Hyde, in 1879. It survived until 1968 when it was demolished as redundant.

Henry Wagner's second church was Christ church, Montpelier Road. This was a slightly more elaborate building as it cost £4,500, of which the vicar, his wife and his sister contributed £200 each. Wagner managed to interest King William IV, Queen Adelaide and, later, Queen Victoria, who each gave £50. The Commissioners for Building New Churches again granted £500 and the Incorporated Society for the Building and Enlargement of Churches a similar sum. The church was designed by George Cheesman junior and built by his firm of builders, Cheesman & Son. For the first time since the building of St Peter's church Gothic was used for the exterior, this time a rudimentary thirteenth-century style. Only the east elevation was exposed, and the chief feature of the building comprised the tower and spire at the north-east corner of the site. The interior still clung to an eighteenth-century arrangement. There were galleries on three sides, although their detail was Gothic, a central three-decker pulpit and a reredos which framed the Lord's Prayer, the Creed and the Ten Commandments. Six hundred and twenty out of the 1,070 seats were free.

The church took less than a year to build and was consecrated on 26 April 1838. The first perpetual curate was the Rev. James Vaughan who ministered at the church for forty-three years. He had been one of Henry Wagner's curates and remained one of his principal associates during the whole of their joint lives. He was an Evangelical in his approach to church matters and was the last Church of England clergyman in Brighton to wear a black gown instead of a surplice when preaching. Christ church was recast internally by Edmund Scott in 1886. It survived until 1982, when it was demolished as redundant after a fire had done considerable damage to the interior. The tower and spire were a great loss to the townscape of that area.

Henry Wagner's third church was St John the Evangelist, Carlton Hill. This was another church built to serve a very poor district. Wagner was so satisfied with the builders, Cheesman & Son, who had erected Christ church, that he turned to them again for St John's, and again the church was designed by George Cheesman junior. But this time the architect reverted to the classical style. Only the south elevation was exposed at the time of building. The church is built of brick, of which the south elevation is painted, with stone dressings. This front has a recessed centre and advanced wings, each flanked by stone pilasters. Above the triglyph frieze a small pediment containing a clock-face crowns the central bay. The elevation is a simple, almost rudimentary composition and reflects the frugal circumstances

25 The original interior of St John's church, Carlton Hill. Drawing by W. A. Delamotte

of the church's construction. Two round blue majolica plaques were added to the flanking bays and a Crucifix to the recessed centre in recent years.

The plan of the interior forms a square with a projection on the south side containing two entrances to the galleries and a vestry between. There is a shallow chancel flanked by pilasters. This originally contained a reredos of two panels framing the Ten Commandments. It has been replaced by a later classical reredos very much in the spirit of the original. This framed a picture over the altar representing Christ as the Good Shepherd and two other scenes from the Gospels. Originally there were a pair of pulpits resting on turned columns with curved staircases giving access to them. But these have been replaced by a single Gothic pulpit of later date. There are galleries with solid balustrades on three sides of the church, of which the south gallery is larger than the others because it projects over the vestry and entrances. The west gallery contains the organ, with the Royal arms. Of the original box-pews only a few remain in the galleries. The Gothic font is of the same vintage as the present pulpit. The original font stood in front of the altar.

The interior of St John's is altogether more elegant than its exterior. Since the demolition of St Margaret's it is, after St George's, the principal classical church to survive in Brighton.

The site cost £908 to buy, which seems surprisingly expensive for a poor and undeveloped area of the town; the construction £3,752. The Commissioners for Building New Churches gave £1,000; the Incorporated Society for the Building and Enlargement of Churches and the Chichester Diocesan Association £500 each. H. M. Wagner and his family were as generous as usual and between them contributed £633. 10s. Wagner again stimulated Queen Victoria to give £50, as was given also by Lawrence Peel and Sir Augustus Dalrymple; the Marquess of Bristol and the Rev. J. S. M. Anderson gave £100 each. When the church was opened there was a debt of £450 still to be raised. Of the 1,200 seats which the church provided, 650 were free. But Wagner realised that in such a poor area very little money could be raised by means of pew rents. Therefore in order to pay the stipend of the perpetual curate he set himself to provide an endowment fund. The Royal Bounty Fund gave £1,400 towards this. The total amount raised was £2,996. 11s. 6d., which produced an income of £93. 7s. 1d. a year. This was well below the sum of £150 which had been set aside for the perpetual curate in the private Acts of Parliament governing proprietory chapels in Brighton. Therefore Henry Wagner had no option but to appoint to the incumbency clergymen of private means to whom a normal stipend was not essential.

The church was consecrated on 28 January 1840. In the absence through illness of the Bishop of Chichester, Dr William Otter, the ceremony was performed by the Bishop of Worcester, Dr R. J. Carr, who had been vicar of Brighton from 1804 to 1824 and was on a visit to the town at this time. The first perpetual curate was the Rev. John Wall Buckley, who only held the office for three years. He was succeeded by the Rev. Spencer Rodney Drummond, who ministered at the church from 1843 to 1861. Both ministers belonged to the Evangelical school of thought.

St John's was a relative failure as a church on the part of Henry Wagner. It proved very difficult to attract a congregation. It was thought that the church had been built in the wrong place. In the second half of the nineteenth century, when churches were entirely associated with Gothic architecture, it was even suggested that the small congregation was due to the classical nature of the building. R. S. Drummond's successor even called it a 'Poor-repelling church'. But the fault lay in the district itself. There were very few people who could afford to pay pew rents, and those for whom the free seats were intended were more attracted by the ten public houses or gin shops and the twenty-three beer shops that the district contained. Some idea of the character of the neighbourhood can be gathered from the fact that it also contained no less than thirteen common lodging houses for the near destitute. The slum character of some of the streets persisted into living memory.

The Rev. Aaron Augustus Morgan, who succeeded R. S. Drummond in 1861, belonged to the High Church movement and introduced ritualist services. But these did not augment the congregation and only produced so much opposition that in 1874 Morgan offered to resign. He actually remained in office until 1879 and became the first vicar in 1874, when St John's was given a parish. At the same time the Ecclesiastical Commissioners provided a further endowment to make the vicar's stipend up to £300 a year. All pew rents were abolished. But although Morgan had a curate, a scripture reader and fourteen district visitors, he was not able to make much impression on the parish.

' On his resignation in 1879 the church was closed for six months as it was found to be unsafe. Scott & Hide of 46a Regency Square estimated that the necessary repairs would cost £2,220. The new vicar, the Rev. R. Edward Hodgson Raines, managed with great difficulty to raise £1,400. The work which was carried out therefore had to be scaled down in proportion. But the roof and ceiling were repaired, the entrances improved, the vestry enlarged and some of the pews replaced. The church was reopened on 12 December 1879.

St John's, Carlton Hill was however distinguished from other poor parishes by one unusual circumstance. It contained two distinguished houses: St John's Lodge immediately adjoining the church on the west and Tower House to the north of this in what is now Sussex Street. These were built by a prosperous merchant named Edwin Adolphus Tarner. He was the son of William and Elizabeth Tarner of Bond Street, London, and was born on 9 September 1808. He married Laetitia, daughter of Edward Tilbury of Marylebone. Edward Tilbury belonged to the family of the coach-builder named John Tilbury who designed the carriage called after him the 'tilbury'. Edward Tilbury, however, was a merchant who had a large warehouse at 35 High Street, Marylebone. He took his son-in-law into partnership, and Edwin Tarner eventually inherited the business. It was then called Tilbury & Tarner.

26 The interior of St John's church, Carlton Hill *c.* 1950

He lived at Tower House, which took its name from the ornamental tower which Edwin Tarner built in the grounds. He owned a fleet of merchant ships trading with America, and it is said that he used this tower to watch for their return. When he sighted them he ordered his carriage in order to drive to the docks in London to greet the ships on their arrival. This story is also told of other merchants at other houses, so it can be questioned, but it is a picturesque legend. Tower House has long since been demolished, but part of the garden still exists as a public open space. The tower is used as a tool shed.

Edwin Tarner also built the terrace of houses between St John's Lodge and Tower House. They were originally known as Patriot Place but are now called Tilbury Place.

Edwin Tarner was succeeded by his son, Edwin Tilbury Tarner at Tower House. In the 1870s he built for the parish a working men's reading room and lending library. His sisters, Clara and Laetitia Tilbury Tarner, lived at St John's Lodge. Laetitia Tilbury Tarner during her long life of ninety-two years (1841–1933) acted more or less as the squire or principal patroness of the parish. Her memorial tablet in the church records that for her and her family 'the fabric of this church, the schools and the welfare of Carlton Hill were a deep and abiding interest . . . a line of benefactors unique in the history of the parish'. When she died in 1933 she left St John's Lodge to Brighton Council. It at first became a children's home, which opened in 1935. But it is now a nursing home which also occupies the whole terrace of houses in Tilbury Place adjoining.

Prosperity never came to St John's church, and about five years ago the church was declared redundant. After a long search for a suitable alternative use it has been taken over by the Greek Orthodox Community and converted for their services.

10

ST PAUL'S CHURCH

All the Brighton churches which have so far been described, except St Nicholas's, were built in the first half of the nineteenth century. But none of them, when first built, had the character of what would now be considered a typical nineteenth-century church. They were in conception and liturgical arrangements of eighteenth-century derivation. They had galleries, box-pews, a prominent pulpit, sometimes even two of these, and a reredos consisting of framed panels of the Ten Commandments, the Creed and the Lord's Prayer. St Paul's was to be a complete break with this Georgian tradition and was to act as a model for all but two of the Brighton churches which were built after it. It was the fourth church built by Henry Wagner in Brighton, but its ideology was entirely that of his eldest son, Arthur Wagner.

It is at first surprising that Henry Wagner chose in this instance to build a new church so close to St Nicholas's on the north west and Trinity chapel on the east. But it must be remembered that immediately to the west of West Street was Russell Street and a congerie of poor streets mostly occupied by fishermen. The 'fishery' as they were called, were then considered a particularly ungodly section of the community, and it was for their benefit that Henry Wagner built St Paul's church.

A Bethel chapel for these fishermen had in fact been built on the site in 1830. This subsequently passed into the hands of the followers of Edward Irving. In 1846 Henry Wagner purchased this chapel, two houses and several shops for £3,000 in order to build his church. His son, Arthur Douglas Wagner was then 22. He was the only child of Henry Wagner's first marriage, to Elizabeth Harriett Douglas. He was born on 13 June 1824 and was educated at Eton and Trinity College, Cambridge, where he read mathematics and graduated in 1846. From his earliest days it was intended that he should take

87

Holy Orders. By 1846 he was not yet ordained, but St Paul's was built with the express intention of being for his ministry. So its character, as eventually realised, represented his ecclesiastical ideas more than those of his father.

The builders were Cheesman & Son, who had given Henry Wagner satisfaction over the building of Christ church and St John's, Carlton Hill. But it did not accord with Arthur Wagner's ideas that his church should be designed by a builder, even if, like Christ church, it was in rudimentary Gothic style. He caused the design to be entrusted to the architect who at that time was the favourite choice of the Tractarian movement then in full spate, Richard Cromwell Carpenter. Carpenter elected to build in the official style recommended by the Tractarians, namely fourteenth-century Gothic or 'middle pointed', as it was then called. The building comprised a nave with aisles and a chancel with organ chamber, vestry and tower to the north of it and a crypt chapel, originally called the chapel of the Holy Spirit, contrived in the slope of ground to the south of the chancel. Exceptionally for a Brighton church, a great deal of care was taken to see that the church was correctly orientated. Therefore as the east end adjoined West Street a long passage was built on the south side to make an entrance at the west end of the nave. The tower was not completed until twenty years later. Behind the church on the west side Henry Wagner built a reading room with a great baronial fireplace. This was intended to be for the use of the fishermen, to lure them away from public houses. But it never proved a success and was later converted into an ante-room or vestry.

The church was built of traditional Sussex material: knapped flints with Caen stone dressings. Building took two years. Without its later embellishments the church cost £12,000. The Commissioners for Building New Churches and the Incorporated Society for Building and Enlargement of Churches again made grants. The remainder of the cost was raised by public subscription, towards which Henry Wagner himself gave £1,475 and his family £1,263. There was accommodation for 1,200 people. Arthur Wagner would have liked to have had no rented pews. But in this he was overruled by his father. Henry Wagner belonged to no particular school of thought within the Church but in such matters as this was rather old-fashioned. Some 460 seats were set aside for renting, and the remainder of the sittings were free. There was at first only plain glass in the windows.

The church was opened by licence on 18 October 1848. The first sermon was preached by the Archdeacon of Chichester, Henry Manning, who was

27 St Paul's church

also rector of Graffham and East Lavington and afterwards Cardinal Manning. The Bishop of Chichester, Dr A. T. Gilbert, consecrated the church a year later on 23 October 1849. Arthur Wagner was not ordained deacon until three months after the church was opened, and priest until a year later. Therefore for the first two years of its existence St Paul's was administered by curates from the parish church. In 1850 the vicar of Brighton presented his son to the perpetual curacy. The church remained in Arthur Wagner's care for fifty-two years.

Over the years Arthur Wagner was gradually able to embellish the church according to his ecclesiological ideas. Most of the original fittings were designed by R. C. Carpenter, for instance the pulpit with its painted wooden panels and tester and the rood-screen in its original form. The latter was then a simple partition of fifteenth-century pattern decorated with figures of saints painted by S. Bell. The same artist painted the scene of Christ in Majesty over the chancel arch. All the stained glass in the main body of the church was designed by Augustus Welby Pugin and executed by Hardman at various dates, often as memorial windows. Amongst the people commemorated were Arthur Wagner's father and mother, his aunt, Mary Ann Wagner, Sir David Scott, Baronet, of Sillwood House, Brighton, the Rev. Gilbert Henry Langdon, the first perpetual curate of All Souls church, and the Rev. Randolph Payne, who was a curate of St Paul's for thirty-two years. The east window in the form of the Jesse tree, which was a gift to the church from H. M. Wagner, was later toned down by the Rev. C. E. Roe to give it an almost medieval appearance. The east window of the south aisle was also similarly altered at a later date. Otherwise the series of windows is complete. The open-work octagonal brass lectern decorated with fourteen statues of angels was the work of James Powell of Powell & Sons of White Friars, London. This was given to the church by an anonymous benefactor who stipulated that the pulpit must cost at least £1,000.

In about 1861 Arthur Wagner took further architectural advice. R. C. Carpenter had died in 1855 and A. W. Pugin in 1852. So Wagner turned to Carpenter's successor as the architectural high priest of the Tractarian movement, George Frederick Bodley. Bodley devised for him a narthex at the west end of the church which connects the entrance passage with the fishermen's reading room. He also designed additions to the rood-screen in the church. These took the form of a traceried canopy painted with flowers. This was actually carried out by one of Bodley's assistants, named H. Ingram,

28 The interior of St Paul's church

aided by one of Arthur Wagner's curates, the Rev. C. E. Roe. The figures
above the screen, by McCullock of Kennington, were not added until 1911.
For the design of a reredos in the chancel Bodley recommended a then little
known artist, Edward Burne-Jones, who later lived for many years at North
End House, Rottingdean. Burne-Jones produced a triptych representing the
Adoration of the Magi, flanked by panels of the Virgin Mary and the Angel
of the Annunciation. One of the Magi in the central panel is a portrait of
Burne-Jones's friend, William Morris. This reredos is now on loan to the

Brighton Museum, but its frame is still in position in the church and is covered by a curtain.

Meanwhile the tower of the church had not been built. When Henry Michell Wagner died in 1870 Arthur Wagner, as his residuary legatee, was in a position to spend more money on St Paul's. For some reason or other he did not give the commission of completing the tower to Bodley but instead to R. C. Carpenter's son, Richard Herbert Carpenter, who is best known as the architect of the chapel at Lancing College, Sussex. It had originally been intended that the tower should terminate in a stone spire. But in 1861 the spire of Chichester cathedral had collapsed. As the tower of St Paul's immediately adjoined the pavement of West Street this made Arthur Wagner doubtful of the advisability of building in stone. Carpenter assured him that the foundations would bear the load, but nevertheless Wagner decided to use a lighter material. Carpenter therefore designed a new octagonal wooden lantern, which was the one actually built. Judging by the surviving prints of the original design, the octagonal wooden version is probably more elegant and certainly more unusual than the original. The tower was built by George Cheesman & Co. between October 1873 and February 1875 and cost £3,120. 0s. 4d. It contains a peel of bells which cost £1,000. The tower and the other embellishments of the 1860s brought the total cost of the church up to £16,000. The tower is really the only portion of the exterior of St Paul's which makes much impact since, like most Brighton churches, the site is much constricted by other buildings.

The interior on the other hand is a splendid composition, making it the second of the great nineteenth-century churches of Brighton. It derives much of its effect from the fact that it is complete with all its contemporary fittings of 1850–61. Other features have been added since, but nothing has been taken away.

However, in Arthur Wagner's own time St Paul's was famous not for the nature or fittings of the building itself, but for the kind of services that were held in it. Amongst those who preached there were Henry Manning, afterwards Cardinal Manning, and John Keble. Pusey and Newman were both friends of Arthur Wagner's but never actually preached at St Paul's. William Gladstone attended services in the church when staying in Brighton.

From 1849 onwards, even before Arthur Wagner's ordination, prayers were held twice a day in the church, and Holy Communion was celebrated every Sunday or Saint's day – which was not then the case in most Brighton

29 The Rev. A. D. Wagner

churches. Later there were five services each Sunday. These services were
of a character which was then known as ritualist, that is to say they were
accompanied by a paid choir dressed in purple cassocks and surplices, and
the officiating clergy wore vestments. Arthur Wagner was always more associated with ritualist than the theological aspect of the Tractarian movement
and was one of the first Church of England clergymen to use vestments and
introduce ritualism into the services. But he never used incense, and the services at St Paul's did not include the more extreme practices that later came
to be used at St Bartholomew's.

This did not prevent the services from being made the subject of extreme
attacks from the ultra-Protestant party within the Church of England. Plac-

ards were paraded in West Street worded 'Morning opera at St Paul's'. The practice which provoked the greatest protests was that of confession. This had been introduced to St Paul's by Arthur Wagner early in his incumbency. But the confessional boxes had been discreetly placed within the enclosed yard to the north of the church, to which the public was not admitted. It was not until the trial for murder of Constance Kent in 1865, when her confession to Arthur Wagner was the central issue of the trial, that the public became aware of the matter. The reaction was immediate and extremely hostile. It produced questions in both the House of Commons and the House of Lords, letters in all the newspapers, both national and local, and a public meeting of protestation in Brighton and even a physical attack on Arthur Wagner. Again in 1873 after the Purchas affair at St James's church the matter erupted when attention was drawn to a notice board in St Paul's church saying that confessions were heard there regularly. Another public meeting of protest was held in Brighton. However, Arthur Wagner cared for none of these things and proceeded on his way undisturbed, the continuation of the practice of confessions included. (For details of the Purchas affair see *The Wagners of Brighton* by Anthony Wagner and Antony Dale (1983).)

In 1873 when the whole parish of Brighton was reorganised St Paul's was given a parish of its own. Arthur Wagner became its first vicar. His first action as such was to abolish all the existing pew rents. Henceforward all the sittings in the church were free. At the time when the five additional churches built by him were administered from St Paul's Wagner employed, at his own expense, as many as five or six curates to help him with the work involved. For the same purpose in 1855 he founded a religious sisterhood named the Community of the Blessed Virgin Mary, which was housed in two houses in Queen Square nearby. This community was expanded as the years passed to include many kinds of charitable work. But originally the functions of the Sisters had been to care for the fabric of St Paul's, to help with the Sunday school and to carry out district visiting. The unfamiliar habit which the Sisters wore and the sinister implications which this suggested in the ultra-Protestant society of the time added greatly to the hostility shown to Arthur Wagner's work at St Paul's during the 1860s and 1870s.

The only addition made to St Paul's during the last twenty years of Arthur Wagner's incumbency comprised four stained-glass windows designed by Charles Eamer Kempe. Two of these are in the crypt chapel of the Holy Spirit, now used as a library, and the other two in the narthex. One of the latter, inserted in 1888, is notable for the fact that it contains figures of Sir Thomas More and John Fisher, Bishop of Rochester. Neither of these men was canonised by the Roman Catholic Church until about forty years later. So these victims of the tyranny of Henry VIII must have been characters who particularly appealed to Arthur Wagner as opponents of that Erastianism which he so greatly disliked. They are perhaps the only representations of these two martyrs to be erected in a Church of England church prior to their canonisation in another branch of the faith.

Arthur Wagner died at his house 'Belvedere' in Montpelier Road, Brighton, on 14 January 1902, aged 77. He had been the incumbent of St Paul's for fifty-two years. He was buried in the Lewes Road Cemetery, Brighton. An alabaster bas-relief in his memory was erected on the north wall of the chancel in St Paul's church.

St Paul's has remained faithful to his memory ever since, both in the maintenance of its fabric and the features which he introduced into it and in the nature of the services held there. But in 1978 the church was 're-ordered' to conform with the liturgical ideas of the time. A detached altar was placed at the east end of the nave. This has communion-rails that were brought from All Saints church in Edinburgh and had originally stood in St Michael's church, Hill Square, Edinburgh. Although they are the only Renaissance feature in the church they fit in extremely well. The Stations of the Cross had been presented to the church six years previously by St Peter's church, Eastbourne, when this building was demolished.

ST MARK'S CHURCH

St Mark's church was opened a year after St Paul's but it was a reversion to the kind of church built prior to St Paul's in the first half of the nineteenth century and is of eighteenth-century derivation. There were two reasons for this. First, the idea of building it was conceived as early as 1837. Secondly, its two principal promotors, the Rev. Henry Venn Elliott and the first Marquess of Bristol, were both old-fashioned people who belonged to the Evangelical movement within the Church of England. As soon as St Mary's Hall school was opened in 1836 H. V. Elliott had been anxious to provide a private chapel for it. He turned for assistance to the Marquess of Bristol, who had already provided the land for the school.

Lord Bristol was the second son of the celebrated Earl-Bishop who, before he inherited the earldom of Bristol had become Bishop of Derry. The Bishop was famous for many things, including the series of Bristol Hotels all over Europe which were called after him, but not for piety. The son had all the piety which his father lacked. He had begun life in politics. After a brief term as British Minister in Berlin in 1797 he had been Under Secretary for Foreign Affairs in Addington's government of 1801–4. His elder brother died in 1796. So when his father died in 1803 he succeeded to the earldom and was created a Marquess in 1826. This inheritance left him free to devote much of his time and fortune to charitable work, including the building of churches. In 1828 he had bought 19 and 20 Sussex Square and built on this corner site one of the finest houses in Kemp Town to the design of Henry Edward Kendall senior. Later he purchased from Thomas Read Kemp 150 acres of land to the north-west of his house including the race-course. It was some extra land adjoining this purchase that he gave to H. V. Elliott for the erection of St Mary's Hall.

Lord Bristol readily agreed to give another piece of land to the south-east of the school in what came to be Eastern Road for the site of a new church, and conveyed this to the trustees of St Mary's Hall in 1838. In addition to the requirements of St Mary's Hall he was also anxious to have a new church nearer than St George's to the original Kemp Town for the benefit of the domestic servants in the Kemp Town houses and the humbler residents of the district. He was nearly 70 at the time and, although in fact he lived to be 90, he was so keen that the new church should be built during his lifetime that he pressed ahead and spent £2,000 on building the shell of the church without having legal backing. There is no precise record of what went wrong, as the twenty-eight letters from Lord Bristol which were once pre-served in the archives of St Mark's seem to have vanished. But the cause appears to have been a misunderstanding about the exact nature of the build-ing which was envisaged. The Bishop of Chichester had given his sanction to a chapel for St Mary's Hall but seems not to have been consulted about a church which would be open to the public. The vicar of Brighton, the Rev. H. M. Wagner, thought that a new church there would be in the wrong place, as new churches should be in the poorer districts of the town. The inhabitants of the original Kemp Town already had their own church in St George's, even though this was about a quarter of a mile away. A new church nearer to Kemp Town would diminish the congregation at St George's, and Lord Bristol was most anxious not to take any step which would be prejudicial to the perpetual curate of St George's, the Rev. J. S. M. Anderson. Whatever was the nature of the difficulties, they delayed the com-pletion of the building by eleven years. The Commissioners for Building New Churches eventually intervened and took over the building.

St Mark's was finally consecrated by the Bishop of Chichester, Dr A. T. Gilbert, on 21 September 1849. The total cost was £4,800, of which H. V. Elliott had given £1,500 and Lord Bristol a further £500. £1,000 was invested in Queen Anne's Bounty as an endowment. The builder was Thomas Sherbourne. Not even H. S. Goodhart-Rendel, who knew more about Brighton churches than anyone of his time or since, was certain who was the architect of St Mark's, but on stylistic grounds he thought that it was probably George Cheesman junior. The similarity of the tower and spire to those of Christ church, Montpelier Road, which Cheesman designed, makes this very probable.

The church is faced with Roman cement in imitation of stone with real stone quoins. It is a simple essay in the Early English manner with lancet windows. The only special feature of the building is the tower at the west end surmounted by a spire. This was intended from the first to have a clock-face, but the clock was not actually inserted until 1867. Three bells by Mears were installed in the tower in 1848 and three more by Mears & Stainbank added in 1867 to provide a chime for the clock. So the church has always had bell-ringing status. Unlike most Brighton churches, St Mark's stands very well and can be seen to advantage on the south side. The building makes an important impact on the townscape.

The interior is less impressive. Originally it was of the usual early nineteenth-century preaching-house pattern. Clustered columns in cast iron support the roof with ornamental brackets of trefoil or quatrefoil design. Some of the oak used in the construction was brought from the estate in Nottinghamshire of Lord Ossulton, who had formerly been Speaker of the House of Commons. There were galleries on three sides supported on fluted columns and box-pews of Gothic design throughout. The galleries were intended for the pupils of St Mary's Hall. At the east end were special pews for the Marquess of Bristol and the trustees of St Mary's Hall, in the south and north corners respectively. There was no chancel. Triple lancet windows surmounted the altar which was set in the usual panels of the Ten Commandments, the Creed and the Lord's Prayer. There were two pulpits, not a pair, of which one stood on a shaped base.

There were 1,019 sittings of which 476 were free. Of the latter, 158 were reserved for the pupils of St Mary's Hall. Four hundred seats were set aside to produce an income of £120 a year for the annual expenses of the church. Pew rents were not finally abolished until 1930, when an endowment of £300 enabled the last of them to be redeemed.

The presentation of the incumbency rested, not with the vicar of Brighton, but with the Bishop of Chichester and the trustees of St Mary's Hall. The first perpetual curate appointed was the Rev. Frederick Reade. He only ministered there from 1849 to 1853. His successor, the Rev. Edward Bishop Elliott, was probably the most important incumbent in the church's history. He was the younger brother of Henry Venn Elliott. He was educated at Trinity College, Cambridge, where he was fourth senior optime scholar and graduated BA in 1816. He was a fellow of the College from 1817 to 1824. On his ordination in 1824 he became vicar of Tuxford in Nottinghamshire and also prebendary of Heytesbury College. Like his brother, he belonged

30 The original interior of St Mark's church. Drawing by W. A. Delamotte

to the Evangelical movement within the Church of England. He ministered at St Mark's from 1853 till 1875 and lived at 11 Lewes Crescent. From 1854 until his death he acted as Honorary Secretary of the Kemp Town Enclosures Committee, more or less in succession to the Rev. James Anderson of St George's, who had held the position from 1828 to 1851. Edward Bishop Elliott died on 30 July 1875 and is buried in his father's grave in the church-yard of old Hove parish church. A tablet in his memory was erected in St Mark's church. This now stands on the north wall of the chancel.

Beside it is a tablet commemorating the first Marquess of Bristol. He died on 15 March 1859 and was buried in a mausoleum in the Lewes Road cemetery, Brighton, the land for which he had given to the town. But at a later date his body was removed by the Hervey family to his ancestral estate at Ickworth, Suffolk. The tablet in his memory in St Mark's church

31 St Mark's church 1987

was erected by the Rev. E. B. Elliott and Lawrence Peel, who was Lord Bristol's neighbour in Sussex Square. The east window is also a memorial to Lord Bristol, the cost of which was raised by public subscription. It originally formed part of the east wall of the nave but was moved eastwards when the chancel was added in 1891.

In 1873, when the whole parish of Brighton was reorganised, St Mark's was given a parish of its own and took over from St George's the role of the parish church of the original Kemp Town.

In 1885 the Rev. H. Newton became vicar of St Mark's. He evidently found the church old-fashioned and inadequate for accommodation. His first step was to build a vicarage on land to the north of the church which was given for the purpose by the third Marquess of Bristol in 1888. Then in 1891 he enlarged the church. He added a shallow chancel and a vestry to the south of this with an organ-chamber over it. The existing galleries were unpopular with the congregation. So those on the north and south sides were removed and the west gallery replaced by a new one straight across the west end of the nave. The organ was not actually moved from the west gallery to the new organ-chamber until 1899. To replace the accommodation lost by the removal of the north and south galleries a south transept was added. A north transept was also projected but never came to be built. The style of the additions was reasonably in accord with that of the original building but with windows in the Decorated style. The name of the architect is not recorded. The additions were made at the expense of the third Marquess of Bristol, who was the grandson of the builder of the church. The reredos of marble and cosmati work was given in memory of Edwin Allum, who died in 1892, and his family. The stained-glass windows in the nave date from 1894 to 1911, the font from 1923. Beneath the gallery is an elegant memorial, in the style of a century earlier decorated with military emblems, to Lieutenant Thomas Butler Ely, son of Major General Ely of 18 Sussex Square. He died in 1900.

From 1911 to 1914 another member of the Elliott family held the living. He was also called Henry Venn Elliott and was a grandson of the founder of St Mary's Hall.

The arrangements of 1891 lasted about eighty years. In the 1970s the south transept was separated from the body of the church and made into a meetings room. The church was declared redundant in 1985, and the vicarage demolished. For a short period St Mark's was administered from St George's church on a temporary basis. But in 1986 it was handed over to St Mary's Hall to form its private chapel. The school intends to remove the west gallery and make the west end of the church into an area for the performance of plays and concerts. It is fortunate that with this transfer the building will continue to be used for one of the main purposes for which it was erected in the first place.

The 1850s saw the opening of two new churches in Brighton and two in Hove. All Saints, Compton Avenue, was the fifth church to be built by the Rev. H. M. Wagner as vicar of Brighton. It was first projected in 1847 to serve the modest streets which were beginning to grow up between Brighton station and Seven Dials after the opening of the London to Brighton railway in 1841. Its guiding spirit was the vicar of Brighton's son, the Rev. Arthur Douglas Wagner. The architect was Richard Cromwell Carpenter. It was built of flints with stone dressings and in fourteenth-century Gothic like St Paul's church. It was in fact in most respects a pale reflection of St Paul's. There was to have been a tower at the north-west corner but, as in other Brighton cases, this was never built.

The Society for the Building and Enlargement of Churches made a grant towards the cost of the building. The vicar of Brighton gave £300. The remainder of the expense was raised by public subscription. The church was not actually opened until 1852. H. M. Wagner appointed to the perpetual curacy his nephew, the Rev. Thomas Coombe, who was of the same High Church persuasion as his cousin, Arthur Wagner. In 1858 Thomas Coombe was involved in a quarrel with his uncle about the nature of the services held at All Saints church and the removal without authority of some of the fittings of the church. The Bishop of Chichester, Dr A. T. Gilbert, had to intervene to settle the matter.

All Saints was a modest little church which never attracted much attention. It was quietly demolished as redundant in 1957.

The second Brighton church of the 1850s was not a Wagner church in the fullest sense, although it was built on land provided for the purpose by H. M. Wagner's sister. Of all the churches in Brighton, St Stephen's has undoubtedly had the most varied history, having stood on two sites: Castle Square and Montpelier Place; and having had five different uses: the ball-room of a hotel, a Royal chapel, an ordinary church and two different secular charitable uses.

In the eighteenth century there were two principal hotels in Brighton. One was the Old Ship on East Cliff, as that part of the King's Road was then called. This was known as the 'Old' Ship from at least as early as 1650. The other was the Castle in Castle Square. The latter was opened in 1755 by Samuel Shergold on the site of a much smaller licensed house. To accommodate the nobility and gentry who flocked to Brighton after Dr Russell published his famous book, *De tabe glandulari*, both hotels added assembly rooms to their existing buildings. The rooms at the Old Ship, which still exist, were built in 1755–6 in the Adam style and were designed by Robert Golden, who also built a set of baths in Brighton for Dr Awsiter. The ball-room at the Castle was the work of John Crunden, the architect of Boodle's Club in St James's Street, London. He was also a follower of Robert Adam. In 1776 Samuel Shergold entered into partnership with Messrs Tilt and Thomas Best. The Castle ballroom dates from that time. In the assembly rooms at these two hotels were held, under the superintendence of an official master of ceremonies in the town, all the fashionable balls and parties which took place in Brighton during the next forty years or so.

The Castle ballroom was also decorated in the Adam style. Its walls were divided into compartments by pilasters, and the spaces between painted with scenes from the Vatican and the Admirander representing Cupid and Psyche and the Aldobrandini marriage. At each end was a recess separated from the main body of the hall by columns. Over their entablature were paintings of Aurora and of Nox. In 1814 an organ by Flight and Robson was inserted in the north recess.

Samuel Shergold died in 1791, Tilt in 1809. By that time the Castle Hotel was somewhat in decline, and in 1814 the ballroom was closed by the tenants, Gilburd and Harryett. King George IV took this opportunity of opening out the view of the Royal Pavilion from Old Steine. He purchased a quarter share in the Castle Hotel in 1815, another quarter in the following year and the remaining half in 1822. He paid a total of £11,210 for the three purchases. He immediately connected the hotel ballroom with the Royal Pavilion by a covered passage which led into the table deckers' room between the banqueting room and the kitchen. The remainder of the hotel was sold off

32 The Royal chapel of the Royal Pavilion. Drawing by W. A. Delamotte

for £5,250 and demolished. The Town Commissioners took the opportunity of acquiring a small strip of land along both Castle Square and Old Steine to widen the road.

The King lost no time in converting the ballroom into his private chapel. There he could hold divine service in which the sermons were given only by his own chaplains or specially invited preachers. By 1821 John Nash was out of favour with the King, and therefore did not superintend the conversion – it is not certain whether any other architect did so. William Tuppen was paid £3,678. 4s. 5d. for fitting up the chapel. In front of the north recess a gallery was built supported on slender fluted columns with pews on two levels and hung with crimson drapery. The Royal pew was in the centre of the upper level – an unexpected arrangement when one remembers that by that time the King had abandoned his apartments on the first floor in the Pavilion and disliked stairs. The wainscoting and the seats were grained, and the latter fitted with horse-hair cushions covered with crimson cloth. The two fireplaces on the side walls were retained in position. There is no pictorial record of the south (liturgical east) end, where the altar stood. But there was an organ there – perhaps the one inserted in the Castle Hotel by Gilburd and Harryett in 1814 – supported on Gothic columns.

In addition to the King's household the chapel seated 400. Admission was by ticket only, signed by the vicar of Brighton. The chapel was consecrated on 1 January 1822 by the Bishop of Chichester, Dr John Buckner, in the presence of the King and his household. The members of His Majesty's Chapels Royal provided the music. The King was present at services in the chapel on all his subsequent visits but did not come to Brighton after 1827. In the succeeding reign the Court came to the Royal Pavilion every year, and William IV and Queen Adelaide always attended services in the chapel. There is a print showing them sitting in the Royal pew on one occasion. Queen Victoria also worshipped there during her various visits up to 1845.

In 1847 the Royal Pavilion was dismantled prior to sale. When the Town Commissioners intervened in 1850 and bought the building for £53,000 to prevent its demolition the Bishop of Chichester, Dr A. T. Gilbert, put forward a claim to the chapel on the grounds that once a building had been consecrated it belonged to the Church. This claim was admitted, and £3,000 was deducted from the sum paid to the Crown by the Town Commissioners.

At this stage the vicar of Brighton's sister, Mary Ann Wagner, offered the diocese both part of a piece of land, on which she had intended to build a house for herself, as a site for the re-erection of the Royal chapel and a contribution towards its re-erection. This land fronted onto Montpelier Place. The offer was accepted and the building re-erected there in 1851 to serve as the place of worship for the Montpelier-Clifton Hill estate. It was again orientated north to south but was given a new south elevation for its principal or entrance front. This is a stuccoed composition in Regency style with four Doric pilasters supporting a modillion cornice and pediment. Above this is a small octagonal lantern. The side elevations, faced with Roman cement and with tall round-headed windows, are similar to the original walls of the Castle ballroom.

Of the original decoration of the ballroom the principal survivals comprise the urn frieze and the pilasters ornamented with scrolls, husks, urns and sphinxes round the walls. Originally these framed paintings but the latter have not survived. The former Royal pew was not retained, but galleries

33 The interior of St Stephen's church 1853. Drawing by W. A. Delamotte

were erected at the north and south ends. Beneath them are recesses flanked by fluted columns with foliated capitals. In the centre of the long east and west walls are semicircular recesses flanked by similar columns. But the altar was not replaced under one of the galleries. It was positioned in the east recess and flanked by a pair of pulpits standing on turned columns with gas brackets lighting them and curved staircases for access. One of these pulpits had started life at the Chapel Royal and was presented to St Stephen's by the Rev. Thomas Trocke, the perpetual curate of the Chapel Royal. The organ stood in the similar recess in the west wall.

The church held 716 sittings, of which 172 were free. It was opened by licence on 25 July 1851, but owing to the illness of the Bishop of Chichester, Dr A. T. Gilbert, it was not consecrated until 11 June 1852. Henry Wagner appointed to the perpetual curacy his nephew, the Rev. George Wagner. George Wagner had been the resident curate in charge of the parish of Dallington in Sussex from 1842 to 1848. Unlike his cousin, Arthur Wagner, he was not a follower of the High Church movement within the Church of England but an Evangelical. He was much influenced by the Rev. James Vaughan, who had originally been one of his uncle's curates and later was for forty-three years perpetual curate of Christ church, Montpelier Road. But by 1851 it was common ground between the High and Low Church movements that Gothic was the only style of architecture suitable for Christian churches. So George Wagner was not attracted to the appearance of St Stephen's church. He was allotted an informal district and worked away there diligently for six years. Amongst other things he founded a Home for Female Penitents which was taken over by Arthur Wagner after his death and absorbed in Arthur's sisterhood of the Blessed Virgin Mary. George Wagner's health was never good and in 1856 he was forced to go abroad in search of a warmer climate. He died of consumption at Valetta in Malta on 10 February 1857, aged 39 and is buried in the Protestant cemetery there. The congregation of St Stephen's erected a tablet to his memory in the north-west corner of the church which is still in position.

After a short incumbency by the Rev. John Chalmers (1857–61) the Rev. Charles Edward Douglas became perpetual curate in 1861. He was the son of Major David Bates Douglas, professor of the Military Academy at West Point in the United States, and grandson of Andrew Elliott, who had been surveyor to Thomas Jefferson. He was educated at Trinity College, Cambridge and had been one of Henry Wagner's curates at St Nicholas's church for fifteen years. He had grand ideas for rebuilding St Stephen's completely and replacing it with a cruciform building in Byzantine style. But these plans were vetoed by the vicar of Brighton. He had therefore to content himself with making minor alterations in the years following 1868. These cost £630 and were paid for by the congregation. The ground floor of the new south front was advanced slightly in order to provide a porch. A vestry was added on the east side. Inside, the walls were painted with scrolled texts (since painted over). The tall Georgian pulpits that had been given to the church by Thomas Trocke of the Chapel Royal in 1851 were replaced by a version more in tune with Victorian ideas. New altar rails, choir stalls and lectern were installed. A new organ by Brindley & Foster was also provided at the cost of £500. After these alterations had been made a surpliced choir made its appearance for the first time. Further internal alterations were made by Sir Arthur Blomfield in 1889 and by Walter Tapper about twenty years later.

34 St Stephen's church 1987

In the twentieth century St Stephen's has had a chequered history. For
a brief period in the 1930s, when the Rev. John Maillard was perpetual curate,
the church was associated with spiritual healing. But after the Second World
War its congregation dwindled. It was therefore closed in about 1970 and
its internal fittings removed. It has since been converted for secular use –
at first as a day centre for deaf people, but this has recently been removed
to new premises adjoining the church of St John the Evangelist on Carlton
Hill. Since 1984 St Stephen's has been used by a housing trust as a day centre
for the homeless.

Unfortunately since it has been in secular use it has been sadly treated.
The north and south ends have been divided off by inelegant partitions. A
sort of bridge at first-floor level has been built across the south end of the
church. The whole building badly needs repair. An application was recently

made to remove the bridge and substitute within the building a kind of two-storey shell or 'pod' to provide some individual rooms. This would have been free-standing and would not have touched the walls or damaged the pilasters or columns of the original decoration. This proposal and the redecoration planned to accompany it would have been a great improvement, but unfortunately it has been withdrawn. It is greatly to be hoped that some other form of restoration will be carried out instead, for the present condition of the interior is deplorable, especially as it has since been damaged by fire.

13

ST JOHN THE BAPTIST'S CHURCH, HOVE

Brunswick Town, Hove, was built in the years from 1824 onwards on the south-east portion of the Wick estate belonging to the Scutt family. In 1825 the Rev. Thomas Scutt agreed to sell the rest of the Wick estate to Thomas Read Kemp, who had some thought of building a Kemp Town West on it. But this never materialised, and in 1830 the land was conveyed to Sir Isaac Lyon Goldsmid, the first Jewish baronet. He is also known by his Portuguese title of Baron de Goldsmid e da Palmeira. In 1830 Goldsmid began to build Royal Adelaide Crescent, as it was at first called, to the design of Decimus Burton. This was to have taken the form of a concave crescent facing the sea. But only ten houses at the south-east corner were built between 1830 and 1834.

No explanation has survived as to why this original scheme was not fully implemented. But it was not until 1850 that Sir Isaac Goldsmid decided to complete Adelaide Crescent. When he did so he scrapped Decimus Burton's original design and substituted a plan for two separate wings of a crescent, as in Lewes Crescent, Brighton, and a square (Palmeira Square) opening out of the crescent on the north. Adelaide Crescent was finished between 1850 and 1860 and Palmeira Square built between 1855 and 1870.

This new estate comprised about seventy houses 'of the first rate' as they would then have been called. There was no church at all near. St Andrew's, Waterloo Street, on the east was not really large enough to take a bigger congregation than the 150 houses in Brunswick Town provided, while on the west the communications to Hove parish church were very unsatisfactory. There was no road along what is now Church Road. It was necessary to drive down to the sea, along the coast road, up Hove Street and back eastwards to the church. It was obvious that the new estate would need a church of its own.

35 St John's church, Hove

For this purpose Sir Isaac Goldsmid offered the diocese a piece of land at the north-west corner of Palmeira Square for the construction of St John the Baptist's church. On 21 March 1851 Hove Vestry expressed themselves in favour of building a church there and resolved to borrow £2,000 from Thomas Thornton towards the expense involved. The church actually cost £4,500. The Diocesan Association for the Improvement of Churches gave £1,000. The remainder was raised by private subscriptions. The foundation stone was laid on 15 April 1852. The architects were William Gilbert and Edward Habershon, brothers and partners.

St John's is a large cruciform building with aisles, a tower to the east of the north transept and a vestry to the east of the south transept and is in Decorated style. Like most of the works of the Habershon brothers, it is not a distinguished building but derives considerable effect from the fact that, unlike most Brighton and Hove churches, it has a very good site and can be seen from three sides without encumbrance. It can perhaps be described as an average Victorian Gothic church. The tower and spire were added about five years after the church was opened. It is fortunate that they were not casualties of time, as in the case of so many churches in Brighton and Hove, because they play a very important part in the silhouette of the church and are the terminal feature of the view of the church along Western Road from the east.

St John's was consecrated on 24 June 1854 by the Bishop of Chichester, Dr A. T. Gilbert. There were 933 sittings, of which 475 were free. The first perpetual curate was the Rev. Frederick Reade, who had been the first perpetual curate of St Mark's church, Brighton, from 1849 to 1853. He lived at 41 Brunswick Terrace. He ministered at St John's for forty years and retired in 1894, aged 85. He died on 15 March 1899. A brass tablet in his memory is to be found in the vestry of the church.

St John's was for many years one of the most fashionable churches in Brighton and Hove. In the early years of the twentieth century a continuous series of porches almost comprising a narthex was added at the west end in what H. S. Goodhart Rendel called 'the Gothic Bungalow style' ('The churches of Brighton', *Architectural Review* 44, 1918). There is a fine east window in memory of Thomas Cooper Smith, who died in 1926. But with the reduction of church attendance during the last twenty years it has become too large for the congregation, so the north and south aisles have been partitioned off. The north aisle is to form a parish hall and the south aisle is St John's day centre.

14

ST PATRICK'S CHURCH, HOVE

In 1851 when the area of the Brunswick Square Commissioners was extended to take in Adelaide Crescent and the site of Palmeira Square the commissioners also assumed jurisdiction over the rest of the former Wick estate, which was the land to the north of Brunswick Square from the Brighton boundary to the site of Holland Road. During the next ten years or so Sir Isaac Lyon Goldsmid proceeded to develop this land by building a number of houses 'of the second rate' on it. It was for the benefit of these houses that St Patrick's church, Cambridge Road was built. The proprietor and first perpetual curate was Dr James O'Brien. He was born in Dublin on 25 July 1810. He was educated at Trinity College, Dublin, and also at Hertford College, Oxford. He eventually became a Doctor of Divinity at Oxford in 1863. He was ordained deacon in 1842 and priest in the following year. Two years later he married Octavia Hopkinson in Chelsea. She was to play a more important part in the history of St Patrick's church than was taken in local church life by the wife of any other perpetual curate in any Brighton church at that time.

In 1857 James O'Brien set about building a new church in Hove. He must have proceeded with the cooperation of the vicar of Hove, the Rev. Walter Kelly, for there was no Act of Parliament. But the building erected was a proprietory chapel. O'Brien obtained a promise of land in what was to be Cambridge Road from Sir Isaac Lyon Goldsmid, and the foundations were laid in July 1857. But when the building was completed fifteen months later Sir Isaac was too ill to sign a conveyance of the land. He actually died in the following April. The church therefore could not be consecrated and had to be opened by licence. But the Bishop of Chichester, Dr A. T. Gilbert, was present at the inaugural service on 20 October 1858. The church was

36 St Patrick's church, Hove

at first called St James's church. In the Brighton directories for 1865–7 it is entered as St Patrick's and St James's. But since 1868 it has always been known as St Patrick's, perhaps to distinguish it from St James's church in St James's Street, Brighton.

The architect was Henry Edward Kendall junior, who designed St Francis's Hospital, Haywards Heath, and remodelled Knebworth in Hertfordshire for the novelist, Edward Bulwer-Lytton. His father, Henry Edward Kendall senior, had been the architect of the Kemp Town Esplanades in Brighton in 1830. The church is built of Kentish ragstone in Early English style. It has a very cramped site, orientated north to south, and is squeezed between

114

two terraces of houses, so only the east elevation can be seen. This is of little distinction. Its chief features are the buttresses to the east (liturgical south) aisle and the gabled clerestory windows. As in the case of so many Brighton churches, there was to have been an octagonal tower, but only the stump of this at the north-east corner of the site was ever built. After such a very unpromising exterior the inside comes as a surprise. The large scale of the plan – chancel with flanking chapels, north-east tower, nave with aisles and an entrance passage or narthex at the south (liturgical west) end – is unexpected. H. S. Goodhart-Rendel scathingly called the church 'spacious without grandeur and ornate without grace' ('The churches of Brighton', *Architectural Review* 44, 1918). But this is rather hard. The effect is quite impressive. The arcades have clustered columns which lead the eye upwards to the unusual hammer-beam roof.

The cost of the building was £13,480. The original fittings were said to have been 'of primitive construction' (*St Patrick's Church, Hove*, Hazel Faulkner and Judy Middleton, 1981). There was at first no stained glass. Most of the pews were rented and brought in an average income of over £1,000 a year.

James O'Brien duly presented himself to the perpetual curacy and ministered there for twenty-five years. His principal interest was in the musical aspect of services, and under his guidance St Patrick's became more famous for its music than any other church in Brighton and Hove until it was rivalled by St Bartholomew's, Brighton in the early years of the twentieth century. There was a surpliced choir which eventually amounted to about eighty men and boys. In the controversial atmosphere which religious practices then evoked this was called by hostile critics 'Paddy's music hall'. O'Brien took particular care with the choice of an organ and consulted Sir John Goss, who was organist at St Paul's cathedral. The instrument which he bought on Goss's advice was made by Henry Willis and was the prototype of the model which came to be known as the Brighton model in Willis's factory. The organ was originally installed in the west (liturgical north) chapel in 1865 and was only moved to its present position in the base of the tower in 1906, when the Lady chapel was made on the original site of the organ. The first organist, who was also recommended by Sir John Goss, was Frederick Bridges, who subsequently went on to be organist at Westminster Abbey. Locally, the best known organist at St Patrick's was Dr Frank Joseph Sawyer, who held the position from 1877 until his death in 1908. He founded the Brighton

Choral and Orchestral Society in 1883 and St Patrick's Oratorio Society in 1904. At his death a stained-glass window was erected in his memory at the north end of the west aisle.

A few embellishments designed by William Butterfield were introduced into the church during James O'Brien's ministry. The first of these was the north (liturgical east) window. This was installed in 1870 and was erected by the congregation as a testimonial to James and Octavia O'Brien. This must be a very unusual nineteenth-century example of a quasi-memorial erected during the lifetime of the people concerned. Butterfield also designed the north-east window of the nave and in 1873 provided the brass lectern. Beneath the eagle at the summit of this is a statue of St Patrick standing amidst Irish peel towers.

In secular affairs James O'Brien was a member of the Hove Commissioners, as the Brunswick Commissioners became after 1873. He was also a Mason and became provincial grand chaplain of Sussex. He lived at 16 Brunswick Place, Hove, and died there on 8 January 1884. He is buried in the church-yard of Hove old parish church in a grave to the south-east of the church marked by a grey granite cross.

James and Octavia O'Brien had no children but they had seven nephews, of whom no less than three were clergymen. James O'Brien had always intended that his successor at St Patrick's should be his wife's nephew, the Rev. Ridley Daniel-Tyssen, and there was a private understanding to that effect between him and the Bishop of Chichester, Dr Richard Durnford. However, in his will James O'Brien made no specific reference to St Patrick's. He merely left his whole estate to his wife. Octavia O'Brien was anxious that St Patrick's should achieve parochial status and enquired from the Ecclesiastical Commissioners whether they would be prepared to accept a gift of the church. She was ready to give the advowson to the Bishop of Chichester provided that Ridley Daniel-Tyssen received the next presentation. Unfortunately she only survived her husband by four months, and during this period there was not time to regularise the position properly. She died on 26 May 1884. Her will again made no specific devise of St Patrick's but did say that Ridley Daniel-Tyssen was left less money than his brother and sister because he was 'the Vicar designate of St Patrick's church by the will of my late husband', although this in fact had not been the case (*St Patrick's Church, Hove*, Hazel Faulkner and Judy Middleton, 1982).

This provision did not satisfy James O'Brien's own nephew, the Rev.

George O'Brien. He contended that any private understanding of the kind in question was invalid and that, as his uncle's heir at law, the church was his property. He brought an action in the court of Chancery against Mrs O'Brien's executors. The principal witnesses in the trial were the Bishop of Chichester, then aged 82, and the equally venerable perpetual curate of Christ church, Montpelier Road, the Rev. James Vaughan. The Bishop testified to the effect that he had regarded Mrs O'Brien as free to dispose of the church as she had wished and had not intervened out of delicacy. Vice Chancellor Bacon gave judgment in favour of Ridley Daniel-Tyssen, and in 1885 he was presented to the perpetual curacy.

He made it his first priority to regularise the position of the church, and it was immediately consecrated by the Bishop of Chichester. By an Order in Council dated 21 August 1885 St Patrick's was allotted an official parish. Ridley Daniel-Tyssen also invited architects of distinction to design individual internal features for the church. The first of these was the reredos, which was erected in memory of James O'Brien. £520 was subscribed by the congregation for this. It was designed by the local architect Somers Clarke. It is of red sandstone with a gilded canopy and represents the Crucifixion flanked by statues of the Evangelists. It was set in position in May 1887. As a memorial to Octavia O'Brien the walls of the chancel were decorated with frescoes designed by Clayton & Bell. These represent Christ in Majesty surrounded by saints and angels. They were executed in 1890–1. The stone and marble pulpit, decorated with seated figures of saints in trefoil-headed niches, was designed by Sir Gilbert Scott and is the only piece of his work to be found in any church in Brighton and Hove except for part of Rottingdean church. It was presented by W. Webster. The alabaster font has no famous name attributed to it and was not erected until 1910. It is an elegant construction of eight three-quarter columns supporting the bowl and topped by a tiered and gilded Gothic canopy.

Ridley Daniel-Tyssen remained incumbent until 1904. In that year he was obliged on account of his wife's ill health to take her to Italy, although she survived until 1930. They later returned to Hove. He died there on 27 March 1917, and is buried in his uncle, James O'Brien's, grave in the church-yard of Hove old parish church. He is also commemorated by a tablet on the east (liturgical south) wall of the chancel in St Patrick's.

Two later vicars also have memorials within the church. On the floor of the north end of the west aisle in front of the Lady chapel is a handsome modern brass in memory of the Rev. Walter Marshall, who was vicar from 1904 till 1919 and subsequently vicar of Christchurch, Hampshire, where he died in 1921. The other memorial is an unusual one. In 1947 Stations of the Cross were dedicated by the Bishop of Lewes, Canon Geoffrey Warde, who had previously been vicar of Brighton. These do not take the usual form of bas-reliefs or sculptures but are framed pictures. They were designed by Louis Ginnett. He was the son of a Brighton circus proprietor named John Frederick Ginnett whose tomb, topped by the marble statue of a horse, is the finest memorial in the Extra Mural cemetery in Brighton. Louis Ginnett was a well-known Sussex artist and a teacher at the Brighton College of Art, now part of the Brighton Polytechnic. Unfortunately Ginnett died in 1946 before he could execute the pictures, and they were instead painted by his colleague at the College, Charles Knight, who was and is an even better known Sussex artist, particularly as a painter in water colours. Six of the fourteen paintings were given in memory of the Rev. Stanley Howard Rutherford. He was vicar of St Patrick's from 1923 till 1945 and was the first vicar who was able to abolish pew rents. The other eight Stations of the Cross were individual private memorials.

In recent years the parish of St Patrick's has been amalgamated with that of St Andrew's, Waterloo Street, and both churches share the same vicar.

15

HOLY TRINITY CHURCH, HOVE

The first expansion of Hove beyond Adelaide Crescent and Palmeira Square was the separate estate of Cliftonville on the west. This was developed from 1852 onwards. We think of Cliftonville today as being the area south of Church Road which comprises Albany Villas, Medina Villas, Osborne Villas, Hove Place and St Catherine's Terrace. But at that time that area was known as Lower Cliftonville. The estate was continued north of Church Road in Upper Cliftonville, which consisted of Hova Villas, Ventnor Villas, George Street and North Place.

These streets were very close to St Andrew's church, then Hove parish church, which was already crowded to full capacity, and the current thinking of the time was that each new estate should have its own church. The idea of building a church in what was then called Hove Fields was to provide such a church for Cliftonville. The man largely instrumental in the erection and adornment of Holy Trinity church, in the words of his memorial in the church, was the Rev. John Fraser Taylor. He was from 1852 to 1864 a curate of Hove parish church. With the approval of the vicar of Hove, the Rev. Walter Kelly, letters of appeal were issued in 1861, and a site in what became Eaton Road was acquired at the cost of £250. The foundation stone was laid by the Bishop of Chichester, Dr A. T. Gilbert, on 7 April 1863. The architect was a local man, James Woodman, who lived at 26 Albany Villas and practised at 17 Prince Albert Street, Brighton. The builder's name was Cane.

Building took just over a year and cost just under £9,000. The church was consecrated as a chapel of ease by the same Bishop of Chichester on 15 June 1864. The building then comprised only the apsidal-ended chancel with its flanking chapels, the nave and the south aisle. It is built of red and

37 Holy Trinity church, Hove

variegated brick with stone dressings. The *Brighton Gazette* of 16 June 1864 described the church as being 'of the Gothic style somewhat inclining to the Lombardic type'. D. Robert Elleray in his *The Victorian Churches of Sussex* (1981)calls it Early English. This is a generous attribution. If it was really intended to be in that style of architecture, then the same phrase could be used of it as H. S. Goodhart Rendel applied to St John the Baptist's church, Hove, namely that 'the details are ignorant beyond belief' ('The churches of Brighton and Hove', *Architectural Review* 44, 1918).

The tower was added in 1866. This serves as a porch and projects rather awkwardly from the centre of the south aisle. It was intended to have a spire, but this never materialised. The spire might have added dignity to the building. The north aisle was built two years later at the cost of £1,200. As completed the church held 850 people. About 150 of the sittings were free. Some pews were subject to only a nominal charge and others were fully rented.

This arrangement was approved by the Bishop of Chichester, although in his sermon at the laying of the foundation stone he had expressed his preference for churches where all the sittings were free. The vicar of Hove duly presented the Rev. John Fraser Taylor to the church as its first incumbent.

The interior of Holy Trinity, with its whitewashed walls, is very plain. There is a gallery at the west end, but the foliated capitals of the stone columns of the arcades are almost the only feature of the church. Being in the Evangelical tradition, it has not acquired with the years any of the more elaborate fittings that adorn the churches inspired by the Tractarian movement. One of the windows in the north aisle is by Hardman. The east window by Ward & Hughes was erected by John Fraser Taylor in memory of his parents. His father had been a naval captain who served under Nelson. On the south wall of the chancel is J. F. Taylor's own memorial. He was incumbent of the church for forty-five years and died on 12 May 1909.

Three years after the death of J. F. Taylor Holy Trinity church acquired its only unusual feature – unique in Brighton and Hove – a wayside pulpit. A small stone preaching recess was added to the south wall of the chancel in 1912. This is said to have been given by 'a soldier and his wife' (*A Short History of Holy Trinity Church, Hove*, 1986).

In the 1920s an attempt made to close the church was successfully resisted. As a result of this skirmish Holy Trinity was given a conventional district but remained part of the parish of All Saints. In 1952 a vicarage, designed by H. Hubbard Ford, was built in the south-east corner of the land surrounding the church. In the following year a parish hall was added to the north-west of the church.

16

THE CHURCH OF
THE ANNUNCIATION

Four new churches were built in Brighton during the 1860s, of which one (St Michael's and All Angels) was an important building. Arthur Wagner did not become fully independent, either financially or ecclesiologically, until after the death of his father in 1870. However, he did manage to build two rather modest churches at his own expense during Henry Wagner's lifetime. The first of these was St Mary and St Mary Magdalene's church, Bread Street.

This was rather near to St Nicholas's church on the west, but it was built to serve the people of the rather poor streets which adjoined the original old town on the north of Church Street. For an architect Arthur Wagner chose George Frederick Bodley, who was working for him at the same time in St Paul's church. The church was a simple barn-like structure of red brick in rudimentary Gothic style. The barrel vaulted roof had tie-beams and arched braces supported by square wooden columns and was pierced with roof-lights. There was no tracery in the windows, no pews, nor any internal fittings of consequence. The building only cost £2,500, wholly contributed by Arthur Wagner. The church was opened by licence in 1862 and was never consecrated. It was administered by curates from St Paul's. Its congregation gradually diminished as the area surrounding it became wholly commercial, and was finally closed in 1948 and demolished two years later.

Arthur Wagner's second church was the church of the Annunciation, Washington Street. This was built to serve another poor district, the hilly streets to the west of Queen's Park which had recently been built or were then in course of construction. The original building is said to have been the work of a surveyor named William Dancy who lived at 33 Montpelier Street, Brighton, but it was so similar to St Mary Magdalene's church that one wonders whether Dancy did not perhaps take over Bodley's design for

St Mary Magdalene's and adapt it to the limitations of the new site. There was in fact no room for a double arcade, so the barn-like building had wooden columns with brackets similar to those of St Mary Magdalene's on the south side only. On the north side the roof came right down to the level of the external wall. Only one elevation was exposed. This was at the east end adjoining the street. This comprised two gables faced with flints with red-brick dressings. Internally there was no attempt at ornamentation, it was just a simple mission church. However, the triple lancet window over the altar at the west (liturgical east) end presumably gave the building the right to be considered as in the Early English style.

The church was opened by licence on the feast of the Annunciation on 15 August 1864 and, like St Mary Magdalene's, was administered by curates from St Paul's. Its first piece of decoration came with the insertion of stained glass in the west window in 1865. The district contained one house, the Attree Villa in Queen's Park, which stood in much the same relation to the church of the Annunciation as did St John's Lodge to St John's church, Carlton Hill. This interesting building in the Italianate style had been built in 1830 by Thomas Attree, a local solicitor who had been clerk to the Brighton Vestry for many years and also held a number of other official positions. He died on 7 February 1863 before the church of the Annunciation was built. But when his widow, Elizabeth Austin Attree, died on 3 November 1865 the west window was inserted in her memory. This depicts the scene of the Annunciation. The centre panel was designed by Dante Gabriel Rossetti and the side panels of angels by Edward Burne-Jones. They were all executed in William Morris's factory.

Unlike St Mary Magdalene's, the church of the Annunciation prospered and by 1881 was proving inadequate for its congregation. Arthur Wagner, who by that time had inherited his father's money, was prepared to sacrifice the existing building and start again, but the clergy and congregation were attached to the old building, so he decided instead to enlarge it. For an architect he turned to Edmund Scott of 46a Regency Square, Brighton, who had already designed for him the spectacular St Bartholomew's church. There was no opportunity to do anything spectacular at the Annunciation. Scott only added a north aisle with wooden columns and brackets similar to those of the south aisle. But in 1882 the church was given from the old parish church of St Nicholas the east window in Decorated style that R. C. Carpenter had inserted in that church in 1853. This was placed in the centre of the

38 The church of the Annunciation

east (liturgical west) end of the Annunciation. At the same time a stained-glass window in memory of Pusey and Keble was inserted at the west end of the north chapel which is called the chapel of the Holy Name. The church as rebuilt cost Arthur Wagner £5,000. It was not consecrated until 1884. As a result of this new status it was given a parish of its own in that year.

In 1892 a tower was added at the south-east corner of the church. By that time Edmund Scott was in partnership with F. T. Cawthorn. The tower was Cawthorn's work. At the same time the east end of the north aisle was partitioned off to form a memorial room or vestry. The adjoining vicarage was built six years later. The Annunciation always followed the ritualist tradition. In 1902 the church was the subject of an attack from the ultra-Protestant party within the Church of England. George Davey presented a petition to the ecclesiastical court concerning the statues, pictures, lamps, candlesticks and confessionals within the church. When the court gave its judgment the removal of these fittings was decreed, although some of them were afterwards returned.

By 1908 it was possible to place two very beautiful Della Robbia figures of the Virgin Mary and the Archangel Gabriel on each side of the entrance to the chancel. In 1924 the Rev. John Coventry Grant Tiley became vicar of the Annunciation. During his incumbency (1924–34) he embellished the interior of the church in several ways. The ceiling of the chancel was painted and decorated with mouldings. The chapel of the Holy Name to the north of the chancel and the organ-chamber to the south were partitioned off with screens of panelling in Elizabethan style surmounted by cresting. The high altar was adorned with a gilded wooden reredos in Spanish Baroque style, designed by Martin Travers. Unfortunately this obscures the lower portion of the Rossetti–Burne-Jones window above. A plain classical pedimented reredos was also placed above the altar in the chapel of the Holy Name, which similarly obscures part of the Pusey–Keble window over it.

17

THE CHURCH OF ST MICHAEL AND ALL ANGELS

At the same time as Arthur Wagner was building his first two independent churches his father, Henry Wagner, was building his sixth and last Brighton church, St Anne's, Burlington Street. Unlike his other five churches, this was not built to serve a poor district. The site was really imposed on him by the wishes of a benefactor named Maria Cook, who had lived in Charlotte Street. Under the terms of her will she left an endowment which would produce an income of £167. 13s. 4d. a year for a new church to be built in the district in memory of her son, the Rev. James Churchill Cook, who died in Malta. Her sister, Mrs Welton, gave a lesser endowment which would produce £29. 1s. 7d. a year and also £150 towards the actual cost of building the church. The remaining sum had to be raised by the vicar of Brighton. Henry Wagner himself gave £2,200 and the Bishop of Chichester £50. The Incorporated Society for the Building and Enlargement of Churches contributed £300 and the Chichester Diocesan Society £40. Wagner entrusted the raising of the remainder to a rich clergyman who had been vicar of Ryde in the Isle of Wight and was prepared to accept the position of perpetual curate at St Anne's for no other remuneration than would come from the pew rents. This was the Rev. Alfred Cooper. He was himself responsible for a gift of £2,000. The cost was £6,956. The foundation stone was laid by Henry Wagner on 16 June 1862. By the time of the opening a year later all but £1,900 had been raised. The church was consecrated on 13 June 1863 by the Bishop of Chichester, Dr A. T. Gilbert. It seated 900 people. Of these seats 500 were free.

The church was built by Henry Wagner's favourite builders, Cheesman & Sons. The architect was Benjamin Ferrey, who had been a pupil of A. W. Pugin. His best work was probably the additions that he made to the Bishop's

Palace at Wells, but his churches are for the most part undistinguished. St Anne's was no exception. It was built of Kentish ragstone and comprised a chancel and nave with flanking chapels and aisles in Decorated style. As in the case of so many Brighton churches only one elevation was exposed, and this made little impression on the narrow street.

The Rev. Alfred Cooper was perpetual curate and vicar of St Anne's for forty-six years. The church had four incumbents in a hundred years, for a later vicar, Canon T. J. James, also served for forty-five years (1910–55). St Anne's was one of those churches which became redundant after the Second World War. In about 1980 it was closed. The tablets in the church which record the circumstances of its erection have been transferred to the narthex of St George's. The other fittings have been dispersed, and the church was demolished in 1986.

The most important church of the 1860s and in fact Brighton's third great nineteenth-century church was St Michael and All Angels, Victoria Road. The area which it serves, now known as the Montpelier and Clifton Hill estate, had been built in the years following 1840. This was never a poor district, but it had no church of its own until St Stephen's was opened in 1851, and then the informal district allotted to that church lay more to the south of Montpelier Place than to the north of it. St Michael's was not one of Henry Wagner's own churches but, living as he did very close by in the new vicarage in Montpelier Road, he was evidently convinced that the church would serve the spiritual needs of the new area and was therefore prepared to sponsor it as a chapel of ease.

The character of the church was more closely, though indirectly, inspired by his son, Arthur Wagner, since the principal promoter of St Michael's was the Rev. Charles Beanlands, who was one of Arthur Wagner's curates at St Paul's. Beanlands was to become the first perpetual curate of St Michael's. He was not the usual type of Brighton clergyman who was able to finance the building of his own church but he had sufficient rich and influential friends for them to take on this responsibility. The principal benefactors were Sarah Windle and her elder sister.

To the north of Montpelier Villas was open land known as the Temple Field with a pond in its north-west corner and diagonally opposite to that an unfinished house known as 'the ruin'. This was the site selected for the new church. The plan was made in 1858 and building began in 1860. The builder was John Fabian. The architect chosen was George Frederick Bodley,

39 St Michael's church

who was working at the same time for Arthur Wagner at St Paul's and at St Mary and St Mary Magdalene's, Bread Street. Bodley had connections with Brighton as his father, Dr W. H. Bodley lived at Merton House, Furzehill, Hove towards the end of his life. Bodley was 31 in 1868, and this was one of his first churches. He produced a design in thirteenth-century style but entirely Italian in feeling. This prompted Mark Anthony Lower in his *History of Sussex* to compare the church to a continental hôtel de ville. It is built of red brick with horizontal courses of stone, and originally comprised a chancel and nave with narrow flanking chapels and aisles. The exterior was very plain, the aisles even stark as they contained no windows. The principal feature was a small fleche on the slate roof. This contained one bell that was brought back from Sevastopol in the Crimea by Captain, afterwards Colonel, Moorsom, who was one of the first churchwardens of the church.

The interior is far more captivating. It is well-lit by the clerestory windows on the south side. The chief features are the tall pointed stone chancel arch and the great squat stone columns on the south arcade with foliated capitals. Bodley was much associated with the Pre-Raphaelite brotherhood which had only been formed about five years earlier. He brought them in to decorate the interior of the church. The members of the brotherhood were so closely interlaced with each other and their styles are so similar that, in the absence of precise records – and in St Michael's case there are none – it is difficult to disentangle individual responsibility. But J. W. Mackail's *Life of William Morris* (1899) specifically says that the roof of the chancel was painted by William Morris, Philip Webb and C. J. Faulkner 'with their own hands'. This decoration can now hardly be seen. The three west windows are usually attributed to Morris and Ford Madox Brown, but Edward Burne-Jones may well have had a hand in them. They were some of the first windows to be made by Morris's firm of Morris & Co. The west window of the south aisle was designed by Bodley himself in memory of his father, Dr W. H. Bodley, who had died on 18 June 1855. The clerestory windows are the work of Worrell. The east window in the form of a Jesse tree was designed by Clayton & Bell and erected in memory of Colonel John Rodger Palmer, who had died on 18 November 1859.

The grey Devonshire marble font was given by a Mr Brown of Aberdeen Lodge, Brighton, and was designed by Bodley, as was the verde antique pulpit that has since been moved to the later part of the church. This was the gift of J. Pearson of Tandridge Park. A very beautiful late fifteenth-

40 The interior of St Michael's church. The south aisle by G. F. Bodley

century Flemish carved reredos was purchased, which was restored by Charles Eamer Kempe at the cost of £400. This shows scenes from the life of Christ and takes the form of a triptych with doors that close. In 1866 Kempe also designed a number of vestments for use at services in the church.

The church took two years to build and cost £6,728. It was consecrated on 29 September 1862 by the Bishop of Chichester, Dr A. T. Gilbert. It held 700 sittings of which 400 were free. The vicar of Brighton duly presented Charles Beanlands to the perpetual curacy. Beanlands was educated at Clare College, Cambridge, and graduated in 1847. He was ordained deacon the same year and priest in 1849. He was a curate of St Paul's, Brighton for the next eleven years. He also held the position of chaplain to the Earl of Crawford and Balcarres. At St Michael's he was from 1862 until 1872 assisted as curate by the Rev. Thomas Walter Perry, who was in 1867 to be a member, representing the High Church movement, of the Royal Commission concerning Rubrics, Orders and Directions for Regulating Worship in the Church of England. Together Beanlands and Perry introduced into St Michael's the same kind of services that were already being used at St Paul's church. There were Gregorian music, the eastward position for the celebration of Holy Communion and a mixed chalice of wine and water, but at first no incense or vestments, although the use of the latter soon followed. In 1865 some of these developments brought Charles Beanlands into trouble with the vicar of Brighton, who, though not himself a member of the High Church movement, was on the whole very tolerant of practices with which he was not really in sympathy. Henry Wagner challenged Charles Beanlands to produce a requisition in favour of the ritual that had been adopted, signed by twelve householder-members of the congregation. Beanlands and Perry were easily able to produce such a requisition signed by no less than 150 people. No further action was taken by the vicar, and St Michael's escaped the violent controversy that characterised St James's church during the Purchas affair and sometimes affected St Paul's and St Bartholomew's churches. This incident must have been one of the very few occasions when the masterful figure of Henry Wagner was defeated in a clash with another clergyman in his parish. (For details of the Purchas affair see *The Wagners of Brighton* by Anthony Wagner and Antony Dale, 1983.)

Charles Beanlands remained perpetual curate of St Michael's until his death in 1898. There is a portrait of him as a young man by Frederick George Watts in the vestry of the church.

No explanation has survived to show why, very soon after the completion of the Bodley church, it was proposed to replace or supplement this with a much larger building. Goodhart-Rendel gives the date of the new project for St Michael's as 1865, but it may have been three years later. One can only assume that the congregation was already so numerous that the existing fabric was uncomfortably cramped for them. Certainly there could be no possibility of providing more accommodation in the narrow blind aisles which, with their coved wooden ceilings, had somewhat the atmosphere of tunnels. But whatever was the reason it did not prove possible to carry out the plan until 1893.

Neither is there any satisfactory explanation of why the new building was designed by another architect, William Burges, who was exactly the same age as Bodley. He was then working in Cork cathedral in Ireland but had not yet embarked on his most famous works: Cardiff castle and castle Coch in Glamorganshire. It has been suggested that the commission was offered to Bodley but that, with the passage of time, he had come to dislike his early work and did not wish to be associated with an extension which was in harmony with his original church. The theory only makes sense if the new design was made in 1893, when the extension was actually built, and not in 1865, which was but three years after the first church went up when Bodley was only 38. The delay in building was so considerable that Burges was not able to supervise the work himself as he died in 1881. The foundation stone was laid by Lady Trowbridge in 1893. The erection took two years. The architect who actually carried out and possibly modified the work was J. C. Chapple.

The narrow north aisle of Bodley's church was demolished. It was replaced by a larger and taller building that was to form the main body of the new church. Beyond this was a new north aisle intended to match in scale the main body of the old Bodley church, which was henceforward to become the south aisle of the completed whole. In materials and style Burges matched the old church reasonably well, but the new building was twice the height of the old one. Outside, owing to the constriction of the site, not much of the new extension can be seen, apart from its great height.

The exterior does not in any way prepare one for the magnificence and the cathedral-like proportions of the interior. There is no further sign of red brick. The whole building is lined with stone or marble. The style is thirteenth-century French Gothic. Above the tall pointed arches of the

41 The interior of St Michael's church. The north aisle by William Burges

arcades are a trifolium of slender black marble columns and a clerestory of wide lancets with roundels over, shielded by a screen of narrow columns that rise through the whole height of the building to the vaulted wooden roof. At the west end is an arcade of two arches forming a narthex with a gallery over it to contain the organ and the choir. In the spandrel between the two arches is a large figure of St Michael carved by a sculptor named Nichols and his son, Tom. The west window above it and also the east window were designed by Lonsdale, who often worked with Burges, and carried out by Worrell. The windows in the north aisle, except for the easternmost one, are by Charles Eamer Kempe.

The new church was not completed to the full scale of William Burges's plans. It was intended to build a cloister to the north of the church on the site later occupied by the parish hall and a tower in the north-west corner that would have been tall enough to be called a campanile. These were casualties of time and money. Inside, further embellishments were intended for the sanctuary. The walls of the chancel were to have been painted. There was to have been a baldacchino over the altar, and predella behind the altar and a sedilia to the south of it. Burges did, however, design the chancel pews, including some miserere stalls. Apart from these there were no pews, only chairs. Burges also designed a large cupboard in the vestry and one chalice. Another chalice was acquired dating from 1596. The church is notable for its plate and its collection of vestments.

Charles Beanlands died in 1898 and was succeeded by Canon R. E. Sanderson. Two years later Sanderson decided to complete the embellishments of the chancel, but not to Burges's plans. This was strange as Burges's drawings are known to have been in the possession of the church until at least 1920. Since then they have unaccountably disappeared. Instead Sanderson entrusted the work to Romaine Walker, an architect perhaps best known for the sumptuous French eighteenth-century decors which he inserted in London houses for Edwardian millionaires. At St Michael's Romaine Walker installed a low wall of Derbyshire marble decorated with cosmati work between the nave and the chancel; also the iron screen of the chancel. He lined the sanctuary with marble (in the place of paintings) and instead of a baldacchino to the altar designed in memory of Charles Beanlands, an elaborate carved and gilded reredos of God in Majesty. The marble altar itself was not placed in position until 1914 and was erected in memory of Mrs Romaine Walker. This was designed by Temple Moore. The rood-screen and Cross were part of Romaine Walker's scheme, but the figures on the screen, which were carved by Peter Rendl of Oberammergau, were added later.

St Michael's was not given a parish of its own until well into the twentieth century. It was then allotted part of the parish of St Nicholas. When All Saints church, Compton Avenue, was demolished in 1957 and when St Stephen's church, Montpelier Place, was closed as a church in about 1970 their parishes were added to that of St Michael's. The parish hall to the north of the church was built in about 1970.

18

ST MARTIN'S CHURCH

1870 was a very important year in the ecclesiastical history of Brighton. The Rev. Henry Michell Wagner, who had been vicar of Brighton since 1824, died on 7 October. With him vanished the last traces of the eighteenth century in Brighton church life. The proprietory chapels of ease that had been built as Georgian or Regency preaching-boxes in the 1820s were by then nearly fifty years old. Some of them were in need of structural repair. All of them were, in their liturgical arrangements, out of sympathy with current ideas. We have already seen how three of them were largely rebuilt in the 1870s. Others were greatly altered then or in the next two decades. H. M. Wagner's death also gave his son, Arthur Wagner, complete financial and ecclesiological independence to proceed with grander schemes than he had been able to promote in the first twenty years of his clerical life. He proceeded in the 1870s to build three imposing Brighton churches, two of which are of the greatest importance, both locally and even nationally.

St Bartholomew's and St Martin's were almost exactly contemporary. The former was opened about seven months before the latter, but it will be convenient to consider St Martin's first because of its personal connection with the late Henry Michell Wagner. During his lifetime the vicar had decided to build another church in Brighton and had set aside £3,000 of his own money for that purpose but had not made up his mind about the site for it nor, on account of age and infirmity, taken any action other than the formation of a building committee consisting of his principal clerical colleagues. On his death Arthur Wagner and his two half-brothers, Joshua and Henry Wagner, at once decided to carry out their father's plan and build a church in his memory. They offered the building committee a choice between a gift of £3,000 towards the cost of building a church on any site in Brighton that they fancied or the Wagners themselves accepting full financial responsibility for building a new church on a site chosen by the family. The committee very naturally accepted the second alternative – a decision which they cannot have regretted as the main fabric of St Martin's church eventually cost £11,398.

The site in Lewes Road that was chosen by the Wagners was a poor district of small houses then largely under construction. Some of them were actually being built at Arthur Wagner's own expense to provide homes for poor people. These streets also adjoined the Roundhill estate on the west side of Upper Lewes Road, which was still without a church since a tentative proposal to build one had not materialised. To serve this district Arthur Wagner had actually built a small mission church in what was to be St Martin's Street. This became the parish school after 1874. Building the new church began in October 1872 and took two and a half years. The contractor was Jabez Reynolds, who had been responsible for much of the Cliftonville estate in Hove. As architect the Wagners deliberately did not choose a famous London name but an old friend of the family. Somers Clarke senior, who was clerk to the Brighton Vestry from 1830 to 1892, had been one of H. M. Wagner's principal associates during all his struggles with a radical Non-conformist opposition in the Vestry. He had a son and a daughter, to both of whom the vicar had left bequests in his will. It was this son, Somers Clarke junior (1841–1926) whom the Wagners chose as their architect for St Martin's. He had been a pupil of Sir Gilbert Scott. He worked at various times in several Brighton churches and was to add an east front to Trinity chapel in 1885, a clerestory to St Nicholas's church in 1892 and a chancel to St Peter's in 1898–1906. He was to become Surveyor to the Fabric of St Paul's cathedral from 1898 to 1906 and architect to Chichester cathedral from 1900 to 1902. St Martin's was his finest Brighton work and perhaps his best work anywhere.

The exterior is fairly muted. It is built of a pleasant brown brick with red-brick dressings in Early English style. It is orientated north to south and, like most Brighton churches, can only be seen from one side, the east – but owing to the width of Lewes Road it is possible to have a better view of this than in the cases of some churches. The plan comprises the usual chancel with flanking chapels and nave with aisles. The latter are both blind and low, which emphasises the great height of the church. At the south-east corner is a gabled porch containing a terracotta plaque of St Martin, by J. B. Phillip, who worked on the Albert Memorial. The original plan provided

42 St Martin's church

for a tower with a saddle-back spire. This was not to have stood detached from the main body of the church but to have extended the whole width of the building and to have risen out of the north (liturgical east) end. In place of this tower only a small bell-arch was built.

The interior is spectacular. The entrance is at the south (liturgical west) end in a portion of the nave set aside as a baptistry and raised five steps above the level of the remainder of the church. From there one has an unrestricted view of the whole as there is no substantial division between the nave and the chancel. No Brighton church had hitherto been built on this scale, and St Martin's is still the largest church in the town. Only the octagonal columns of the aisles are of stone. The rest of the arcades are of red brick with a narrow trifolium and a clerestory of lunette windows above. The roof is painted with armorial bearings.

43　The interior of St Martin's church

Part of the great effect of the church derives from the fact that all its internal fittings were designed by the architect, Somers Clarke, and executed under his supervision. Chief amongst these is the reredos, constructed by J. E. Knox. This contains twenty pictures and sixty-nine statues. The paintings are the work of H. Ellis Wooldridge. The statues were carved at Oberammergau by Josef Mayr (a former Christus in the Passion play). It is said that three of the statues were likenesses of the Rev. Henry Michell Wagner, of his grandfather, the Rev. Henry Michell, and of his father-in-law, Joshua Watson, the leader of the pre-Tractarian High Church movement. But they are too highly placed to be recognisable. The present marble altar below the reredos was not installed until 1949.

Next in importance, and also by Somers Clarke, is the pulpit which dates from 1880. It derives from the Sacrament House in the church of St Sebald in Nuremberg and has affinities with the bishop's throne in Exeter cathedral. It is also the work of J. E. Knox. The base is inlaid with olive-wood brought back from the Mount of Olives by Henry Wagner on one of his journeys. The font in the baptistry at the south (liturgical west) end was not erected until 1907. It is of Sussex marble inlaid with other marbles and precious stones that were also brought back by Henry Wagner on other journeys from Cairo, Rome, Ostia and Pompeii. The very tall tiered oak canopy echoes the pulpit. It cost £400 and again was the gift of Henry Wagner.

Twelve of the stained-glass windows in the clerestory were also given by him, as was the east window in memory of his mother, Mary Sikes Wagner, whom he had never known, and his aunt, Mary Ann Wagner, who had brought him up. This window was designed by James Powell of Powell & Sons, White Friars, London. The figures on the rood-screen were not erected until 1909 in memory of Mary Ellen Little.

The church was consecrated on 1 May 1875 by the Bishop of Chichester, Dr Richard Durnford. It held 1,500 people. All the sittings were free. Together with all the fittings the building probably cost as much as £15,000. The vicar of Brighton, the Rev. John Hannah, appointed to the perpetual curacy the Rev. Robert Ingham Salmon, who had looked after the temporary church in St Martin's Street since 1872. He had been educated at Exeter College, Oxford, and served as a curate at Morchard Bishop in Devonshire (1861–2) and at the church of St Michael and All Angels in Paddington from 1862 to 1872. He had only to wait six months before becoming a vicar, for St Martin's was allotted a parish of its own in October 1875. He ministered at the church until 1888, when he became rector of Barcombe in Sussex. During his ministry the services at St Martin's were not of the ritualist nature that characterised those of St Paul's although they came to be so in the next century.

During the hundred years since its consecration St Martin's has maintained two lasting connections, both of which have left visible records in the church. The first of these was with Preston Barracks. This was situated in the parish about a quarter of a mile up the Lewes Road to the north. On the east (liturgical south) side of the chancel, balancing the organ-loft on the other side, is a small gallery. This was built to enable part of a military band from the barracks to take part in occasional services. On many occasions this was used for that purpose when troops attended at the church until the barracks were closed about ten years ago. The low marble wall of the chancel with the wrought iron gates in the centre were given to the church by the Fourth Royal Irish Lancers, in memory of their comrades who were killed in action in the Egyptian Campaign of 1882 and in the Nile campaign of 1884–5. At the same date (1885) the Fourth Dragoon Guards, who had a particular connection with St Martin's, were withdrawn from Preston Barracks and in the following year erected a memorial of mosaics and tiles in the north-east corner of the nave in memory of their members who had been killed in the same Sudan campaign of 1884–5.

The second lasting connection of the church is with the Wagner family. When St Martin's was first built a tablet with a Latin inscription was erected in the south-west corner of the chancel, recording that the church had been built in memory of the Rev. H. M. Wagner by his three sons. When Henry Wagner inserted the east window in memory of his mother, Mary Sikes Wagner, and his aunt, Mary Ann Wagner, he recorded their deaths in a similar tablet in the north-east corner of the chancel. When Arthur Wagner died on 14 January 1902 a third tablet was installed to the south of the last one. The balancing space in the north-west corner of the chancel was used to record the death of Henry Wagner, who had lived at 7 Belvedere Terrace, Brighton since 1921. He died there on 24 April 1926. He bequeathed two pictures by Urbertino to St Martin's church.

1925 had been the silver jubilee year of the church's consecration. A special collection of £225 had been made on that occasion. The parish decided to use this money to embellish the Lady chapel in memory of Henry Wagner. The existing carved reredos was found to be decayed and affected by dry rot. It was replaced by a picture of the Virgin and Child set in an elaborate Renaissance frame surmounted by the arms of the diocese of Tours, of which St Martin was bishop.

Henry Wagner was the last of his line in the Wagner family, as neither he nor his two brothers ever married. But his heir was his cousin, Orlando Henry Wagner, great-grandson of his great-uncle, Anthony Wagner. This branch of the family has continued the connection with St Martin's. When Orlando Wagner died in 1956 and his widow, Monica Wagner, in 1971, their son, Sir Anthony Wagner, who was Garter King of Arms from 1961 to 1978, erected a tablet in their memory on the north wall of the Lady chapel.

19

ST BARTHOLOMEW'S CHURCH

St Bartholomew's church, Anne Street, is the most outstanding and probably the most famous Brighton church. It was exactly contemporary with St Martin's but was the sole responsibility of the Rev. Arthur Douglas Wagner without the cooperation of his two half-brothers. The district west of London Road was an area where he thought missionary work was necessary. So in 1868 he had built in Providence Place a school for 400 children and a temporary church holding 350 people. This church was a barn-like brick structure not dissimilar to Bodley's St Mary and St Mary Magdalene's, Bread Street. It survived until 1939, when it fell a victim to a fire. After the construction of the main church it was always known as 'the little church'.

As soon as Arthur Wagner had inherited his father's estate he determined to replace this church with a more permanent building and moreover to give this the maximum of magnificence with the minimum of cost. As in the case of St Martin's, he chose to design it a local architect, Edmund Scott, who was then quite unknown. Scott was born in 1828 and came to Brighton in 1853. He practised at 46 Regency Square, first with another architect named Suter, and later at different times with other partners named Hyde and F. T. Cawthorn. But at this period he was on his own. He was what H. S. Goodhart-Rendel called a 'rogue architect' in that he belonged to no school or movement and had few predecessors or successors. He had a fairly extensive church practice in and around Brighton, but most of his work was of a very modest character. St Andrew's, Portslade, was an early work (1863) but is a very insignificant building in Early English style. In Brighton itself he rebuilt St James's church in St James's Street (1875) and was responsible for St Saviour's church, Ditchling Road (1885), although the tower of the latter was never built. Both churches have been demolished since the Second

World War, although the magnificent reredos from Chichester cathedral, which was inserted in St Saviour's in 1909, was salvaged and moved to the disused church of All Saints, Portfield, Chichester, now a museum of mechanical pianos and organs. Neither St James's nor St Saviour's church was of special distinction.

Scott's other work in Brighton comprised alterations to the interior of St John the Baptist's, Carlton Hill in 1879, the addition of a chancel to All Souls, Eastern Road in the same year, the enlargement of the church of the Annunciation, Washington Street in 1882 and the recasting of the interior of Christ church, Montpelier Road in 1886. Apart from St Bartholomew's, Brighton, his best building is probably St Botolph's church, Heene, West Worthing (1872–9). This is a large and quite impressive aisled Gothic church, built of an unusual combination of materials for a church – cobbles (instead of flints) and red brick. But it gives no inkling of the majesty which, at the very same time, he was providing in St Bartholomew's. As far as great works go, Edmund Scott remained a one-work architect. The only explanation of the contrast between the splendour of St Bartholomew's and the modesty of Scott's other works would seem to be that he never again found a client who was prepared to disregard expense. Probably Arthur Wagner also had a considerable part in the design of the church which he commissioned.

The first project for the church, which received municipal approval on 7 June 1871, differed somewhat from the executed plan. It provided for a church of thirteen bays and a school in a single continuous building 322 feet long. This was subsequently amended to reduce the length of the church from thirteen to eleven and a half bays and to provide a courtyard between the church and the pre-existing school. Even as altered, the church would only have been 46 feet wide and 41 feet 9 inches high to the wall-plate, which was about half the height actually built. Between the church and the existing houses in London Street on the west was to have been a narrow triangular space forming a vestibule and four vestries. The foundation stone of this building was laid on 8 February 1872.

Very soon after building began Arthur Wagner evidently changed his mind and decided to have something much more magnificent. New plans were submitted on 16 September 1873 for a church which would be 59, instead of 46, feet wide, 170 feet long, 90, instead of just under 42, feet high to the wall-plate and 135 feet high to the ridge of the roof. This would make the building four feet higher than Westminster Abbey and even today prob-

44 St Bartholomew's church

ably the tallest church in England. Bearing in mind that St Peter's church, which had been built by his father in Portland stone nearly fifty years before, had cost £25,000, Arthur Wagner decided to build in brick: red stock bricks, relieved with courses of stone. The roof originally had a variegated pattern of red and black tiles but lost these when the church was retiled in 1930. The style is early Italian Gothic, but Edmund Scott was also probably influenced by the work of James Brooks and G. F. Bodley.

Construction took a year and seven months. The contractors were Stenning & Co. of Brighton. The cost was £18,000. Even the plan of September 1873 was not fully carried out. This showed eleven and a half bays, but only nine were built. Sawyer's *The Churches of Brighton* (1883) spoke of an intention to build transepts, but this was manifestly impossible as the east wall of the church abuts onto Providence Place. The *Brighton Gazette* of 10

144

September 1874 mentioned a proposal for an apsidal chancel and 'a pretty spire', but the deposited plans show nothing of the kind. However, the north end, which is the liturgical east end as the church was orientated north to south, was definitely not finished and on three occasions since then plans have been made to complete it.

The principal features of the exterior are the rhythm of buttresses at clerestory level on the long east and west sides and the great round window on the south front – one of the largest circular windows in existence. But the church of course derives its main effect from its great height. This can be seen to better effect today than when it was first built for the church was then surrounded by small houses which obscured the lower part of the building. These houses entered into the saga of the church's history as some of the owners of those on the west side claimed that the great height of the building caused their chimneys to smoke. Arthur Wagner promptly bought up the houses in question and reduced their rents. One wonders whether, knowing his wealth and benevolent disposition, it was a put-up job on the part of the claimants. Today the site around the church has been largely cleared, except for the horrible school on the west side. So St Bartholomew's can be seen to its full advantage.

As soon as the very unusual nature of the building and in particular its great height became apparent a storm of protest arose. It was called such names as 'the barn', 'Noah's Ark', 'Wagner's folly'. All aspects of the building and its promotors were criticised. Ridiculous reports were circulated about the building, such as that it contained a circular staircase of 175 steps leading to 58 dark cells. What could be their purpose? The reference was presumably to the portions of the narrow triforium where this passes through the main pillars of the church. Even the Town Council reacted unfavourably. It was clear from their proceedings that, when they passed the plans of the church, they had not realised how tall this would be and that, when they saw it on the ground and it was too late to refuse permission, they regretted that they had given consent. They discovered that the church, as erected, was actually two feet higher than the plans had shown. The Council then discussed whether they should take proceedings against Arthur Wagner for this discrepancy but resolved by 21 votes to 11 that, as the maximum fine that could be imposed was £2, this was not likely to make much impression on a man who had just spent £18,000 of his own money on building the church. Therefore they decided to take no action.

45 The interior of St Bartholomew's church

The interior of St Bartholomew's is even more unusual than the exterior. Again it is the great height that is the dominant feature. In reference to this, Arthur Wagner used to say that, measured by the standard of the cubic feet of air space, it was the cheapest church ever built in England. The brick-work of the walls is everywhere exposed. The church forms one vast hall with no aisles and no division between nave and chancel. The side walls are divided into tall narrow pointed arches which form side-chapels flanked by brick piers. Above is a very shallow triforium with narrow lancets and a clerestory of wider lancets flanked by the thin brick pilasters that support the barrel-vaulted wooden roof.

In Arthur Wagner's day the interior did not present the splendour that it does today because some of its finest features were not inserted until after his death. The most important original fitting was the great Cross, 30 feet high, on the north (liturgical east) wall. This is made of white encaustic tiles let into the wall and then incised with a figure of Christ and painted by S. Bell, who also worked at St Paul's church. Below this Cross was originally a huge dorsal that is said to have been designed by George Edmund Street. This took the form of a triptych of panels of material, of which the centre panel was higher than the others and was surmounted by a canopy bearing the words 'Sanctus, Sanctus, Sanctus'. The sanctuary then, as now, was raised above the level of the main body of the church by two short flights of steps. The altar at the head of these steps was also painted by S. Bell.

It was intended that all sixteen of the lancet windows should contain stained glass, but only four were actually commissioned. These were the work of Walter Tower, the cousin and partner of Charles Eamer Kempe. Another original feature is the Stations of the Cross. These were brought from Bruges in 1881 and are of stone and carved wood, set into the brick wall-piers. They must be amongst the earliest examples of Stations of the Cross to be erected in any Anglican church. So must be the confessional-boxes, which were installed in some of the recesses of the nave in the preceding year. They have domed tops which are curiously reminiscent of the Royal Pavilion, being surmounted by miniature oriental pavilions bearing a cross. The original pulpit was of stained wood, standing on open legs and with a flat sounding-board over it. The original font was the gift of the architect, Edmund Scott.

St Bartholomew's was opened by licence on 18 September 1874. It could seat 1,500, and all these seats were free. It was the first church in Brighton of which this was true from the date of its opening. The building also had the innovation of being lit by gas from tall L-shaped brackets hanging from triforium level. There was a choir of between 50 and 60 people at services. At the third service of the opening day the Bishop of Chichester, Dr Richard Durnford, was present and preached a very tactful sermon, appealing for toleration of unfamiliar features or practices that could not be called superstition.

For another six years the church was administered as a chapel of ease from St Paul's and was largely financed by Arthur Wagner, although the Ecclesiastical Commissioners gave an endowment of £150 a year. The first priest in charge was the Rev. Arthur Payne, who was one of Arthur Wagner's curates and had looked after the mission church since 1870. St Bartholomew's was not given a parish of its own until 1881. The first vicar was therefore the Rev. Thomas William Sands Collis, who had also been one of Arthur Wagner's curates at St Paul's but from 1865 to 1874 was vicar of St Paul's, Knightsbridge, London. He ministered at St Bartholomew's from 1879 to 1895. The church was not consecrated until 1887 by the same Bishop of Chichester.

In 1895 the Rev. Arthur William Carew Cocks became vicar of St Bartholomew's. He set himself to embellish the interior of the church. Edmund Scott died that year, so for his architect Arthur Cocks chose Henry Wilson. The latter had started life in the office of J. Oldrid Scott and had later worked first for John Belcher and then for J. D. Sedding. When Sedding died in 1891 Wilson took over Sedding's practice. After he became editor of the *Architectural Review* in 1896 and later also a lecturer at the Royal College of Art he turned away from architectural work and eventually was to become wholly a metal-worker and jewellery designer. In that capacity he served as president of the Art Workers Guild in 1927. His designs for St Bartholomew's were his last important architectural commission.

He produced a full-dress scheme for completing the north (liturgical east) end of the church. Drawings of this scheme have survived in the Royal Institute of British Architects. In the place of the vestry behind the high altar he proposed to extend the church by three bays to form a Lady chapel with a barrel vault decorated with a pattern of gold criss-cross on a blue ground. The straight end of the chapel was to have been decorated with a huge mosaic, 30 feet high, of the Madonna surrounded by heavenly souls. The chapel would have been separated from the main building by three arches filled with iron grilles and marble tracery in the heads. This scheme was never carried out, no doubt for financial reasons. There was no longer a Wagner–Maecenas to subsidise embellishments of such a kind. Arthur Wagner did not die until 1902, but in his last years he was infirm and not capable of doing business.

Henry Wilson did, however, design five features for the church which were actually carried out. The first of these was for the improvement of the sanctuary in 1899–1900. In the place of the dorsal behind the high altar Wilson built a Byzantine baldacchino 45 feet high, which cost £2,000. This is of red marble with capitals of interlaced vine pattern and a green marble canopy. The ceiling of the latter is inlaid with gold and mother-of-pearl. The altar of 1874 by S. Bell was replaced under the baldacchino by a tabernacle of beaten silver designed by Wilson. Above this is a gradine or shelf of white marble to support six large candlesticks and a Crucifix. Unfortunately Wilson's original Crucifix was removed to the Lady altar in 1912 and replaced by one designed by McCulloch of Kennington. An afterthought of 1905 was the very beautiful brass railing in Art Nouveau style inset with blue enamel. To this was added three years later two large columns of white Tuscan marble supporting giant candles.

Wilson's second contribution to St Bartholomew's was the Lady altar in 1902. This replaced the altar designed by Charles Eamer Kempe in 1888, which was removed to St Alban's church, Coombe Road, Brighton. The frontal of the new one is of repoussé silver plate on copper. The Crucifix above is the one which Wilson originally designed for the high altar and which was transferred here in 1912.

Next in importance to the baldacchino is the pulpit, which Wilson designed in 1906. This is of green Irish marble supported on six red African marble columns standing on a base of black marble from Tournai. A miniature curved staircase is cunningly contrived behind the columns. The upper level is backed by a curved screen of alabaster, on which hangs a Crucifix. This is rather out of scale with the rest of the pulpit as it was originally made for the much smaller original pulpit of 1888.

At the same time as the new pulpit was erected an abortive attempt was made to install a new organ in the north-west corner of the church. Once half-built it was seen that this would obscure the view of the whole church in one glance. This has always been a special feature of the building, so the work was hastily removed and a gallery built by Wilson at the south (liturgical west) end of the building to house the organ. This has a central console with the pipes grouped on each side of it. The gallery is large enough to seat a choir and orchestra of 150. An orchestra was an addition sometimes made to services at that time.

Henry Wilson's last contribution to the church, in 1908, was the font. The second recess from the south on the east side of the church had been set aside as the baptistry. Three circular black marble steps support an octagonal basin of green marble panels set in frames of beaten copper with a flat wooden cover.

Henry Wilson's work at St Bartholomew's adds so much to the splendour of the church that Sir John Betjeman once said that one could almost expect the clergy to make their entrance on elephants. He also called the building 'the cathedral of the London to Brighton and South Coast religion'.

In 1910 the Rev. A. W. C. Cocks left not only St Bartholomew's church but also the Church of England for the Church of Rome. His successor, the Rev. Henry Ross (1911–18) did not continue to employ Henry Wilson but made another project to complete the church at the north end. The name of the architect has not been recorded. But the plan was to build a new chapel over the existing single-storeyed vestry, to form a new high altar and to insert stained glass by J. C. Bewsey in the great circular window at the south end of the church. These plans were no doubt amongst the many to which the outbreak of war in 1914 put an end. But one thing was actually carried out in 1912 – the mosaics behind and flanking the baldacchino. These were designed by F. Hamilton Jackson, an art-worker in the Dixon-Paul Cooper circle at Birmingham. They depict Christ in Glory surrounded by the Saints. These mosaics have on the whole not been well received. H. S. Goodhart-Rendel, writing only six years after they were installed, called them 'of almost incredible feebleness' ('The churches of Brighton and Hove', *Architectural Review* 44, 1918). He was probably comparing them in his mind's eye with the larger version of mosaics which Henry Wilson had designed for his Lady chapel, which was never built. But now that they have been in position for more than seventy-five years since he wrote they have come to take their place in the church and can be held to add lustre to the majesty of the sanctuary.

When the First World War was over a third plan was made to complete the north end of the church. Henry Ross's successor, the Rev. Gilbert Gervasse Elliott (1918–35) – who was nothing to do with the Elliott family of St Mary's and St Mark's churches – asked Sir Giles Gilbert Scott to consider the problem. Scott produced a plan to add a polygonal apse of one and a half bays but retaining the existing baldacchino. This project never proceeded any farther no doubt again for financial reasons, and in 1930 whatever money was available had to be spent on retiling the vast roof of the church. But one reminder of Sir Giles Gilbert Scott remains in the church in the form of a statue designed by him behind the font. This is of St John the Baptist and was executed by R. D. Gough in 1925.

One later vicar deserves special mention. This was Canon Charles Walsham Hutchinson the incumbent from 1947 to 1961. From 1925 to 1943 he had been vicar of St John the Evangelist with All Saints, Waterloo Road, London. He became a canon of Southwark cathedral in 1943 but spent the next four years as chaplain to the British Embassy at Istanbul. The Old Vic Theatre was in his London parish, and this led him to have many theatrical connections. In Brighton he held the almost self-invented honorary post of chaplain to the Theatre Royal. In his time the clergyhouse of St Bartholomew's was at 87 London Road, the elegant villa designed by Wilds and Busby about 1825 which is now the Brighton vicarage.

After St Bartholomew's and St Martin's Arthur Wagner built one more Brighton church in the 1870s, his fifth and last. This was the church of the Holy Resurrection in Russell Street. Throughout the nineteenth century a great many of the houses in the Russell Street area were occupied by fishermen. For some reason or other the 'fishery' were thought to be largely outside church life. Arthur Wagner's father had built St Paul's church in West Street in the hope of attracting fishermen away from the public houses of the district. But his aim had not been realised. Arthur Wagner seems to have thought that St Paul's had proved too large and too grand and that its congregation became too fashionable for them. If he built another much smaller and simpler church specially for the fishing community this might attract them to attend services, despite the fact that the new site was so very near to St Paul's.

He at first intended that the church should be called the church of the Transfiguration. For his architect he chose Richard Herbert Carpenter, who had designed for him the octagonal lantern of St Paul's. Like Edmund Scott, R. H. Carpenter was really a one-work architect, as no other building designed by him came anywhere near the quality of his Lancing College chapel. The new church was built in 1876–7. As soon as work began Arthur Wagner ran into trouble. An adjoining brewery objected to the proposed height of the building and successfully claimed the right of ancient lights. Arthur Wagner was not to be put off by this and decided that, if he could not build upwards, he would do so downwards. He had the ground excavated to such a depth that the church was approached down thirty-two steps. As a result the exterior was a somewhat featureless red-brick building. But the interior, which was of stone, was a rather splendid essay in thirteenth-century Gothic with aisles and a dual chancel arch.

As soon as it was completed another difficulty arose. Arthur Wagner had a fixed objection to the consecration of churches. This was a prejudice that was shared by many Tractarians. They thought that consecration made it easier for the State to intervene in the life of the Church. The Bishop of Chichester, Dr Richard Durnford, on the other hand, had an equally strong objection to churches not being consecrated. In the case of the church of the Resurrection he was fortified in this view by the knowledge that St Bartholomew's had not been consecrated before it was opened and was in fact not consecrated until seventeen years later. He therefore refused to issue a licence for the new church to be opened without consecration. Despite the intervention of Dr Edward Pusey on Arthur Wagner's behalf the Bishop held firm, and Wagner had to give way. The church was consecrated and opened for worship in 1878.

During Arthur Wagner's life the church was financed by him and administered from St Paul's as a chapel of ease, but it is unlikely that it succeeded in attracting the fishing community to services. When Arthur Wagner died in 1902 the church became a problem and was closed for services ten years later. It was then converted into a wholesale meat store. Owing to the semi-subterranean nature of its construction it was almost a secret building, and few people were aware of its existence or history. It was demolished without protest in 1966.

20

ST BARNABAS'S CHURCH, HOVE

In 1865 what is now Hove Station was opened. It was then called Cliftonville Station, hence the name still borne by the public house to the south of it. When the land between Palmeira Square and Cliftonville was laid out by the Stanford Estate as the Avenues and at first called West Brighton, the station was renamed West Brighton. After these Avenues were absorbed in the generality of Hove the name was again changed to Hove Station. The streets to the south of the station between Conway Street and Upper Cliftonville grew up in the years following 1865. By 1880 the development had reached Sackville Road but had not gone beyond that line. The population of the area had increased by about 10,000 in the previous ten to fifteen years. The Rev. Thomas Peacey, who had become the first vicar of Hove without Preston in 1879, felt that the people of these new streets needed spiritual provision of their own.

The first step was the starting of a mission church in a corn-loft in Conway Street. But on 14 March 1881 Thomas Peacey called a public meeting in the Town Hall to consider the question of erecting a permanent building. This meeting decided to build on a site offered by Messrs Beves on the west side of Sackville Road between what came to be Byron Street and Coleridge Street. A second meeting, with the Bishop of Chichester, Dr Richard Durnford, in the chair, was held on 2 April in the Ice Rink to discuss the question of finance. By June £2,500, which was estimated to be about a third of the sum needed, had been raised.

For the architect Thomas Peacey chose John Loughborough Pearson, with whom he was already in touch over the separate question of building a vicarage for the parish church in Hove. The foundation stone of St Barnabas's was laid by the Bishop of Chichester on 27 May 1882. The church was built

46 St Barnabas's church, Hove

of knapped flints with red-brick dressings and quoins in the then prevailing Early English style. It is a cruciform building with an apsidal-ended chancel, a nave with aisles, and a gabled porch at the north-west corner, which was originally the main entrance. There was to have been a tower at the south-west corner but, as in the case of so many Brighton churches, only the base of this, in white brick, was ever built. Pearson was probably the finest architect of Anglican churches in the nineteenth century. Some of his larger churches are of considerable magnificence. St Barnabas is not amongst these. Pearson himself called it 'one of my cheap editions'. It is nevertheless a fine example of a moderate sized flint and brick church in thirteenth-century style and far superior to some of the very simple churches which Pearson had built in Yorkshire during his early days. Unfortunately, the main view of the church, which was from the south-east, has been permanently blocked off by the building in 1893 of the vicarage (whose architects were Clayton and Black) and to a lesser extent the parish room to the west of this.

The construction of the church took just over a year and cost £6,500, in addition to the sum of £1,500 which had been paid for the site. All the money had been raised before the church was opened. It was consecrated by the Bishop of Chichester, Dr Richard Durnford, on 11 June 1883. It held 834 people. All the sittings were free from the beginning. The first incumbent was the Rev. Alfred George Lovelace Bowling, who held the living until 1897. St Barnabas was allotted a parish of its own by Order in Council in 1884.

The interior of the church originally had few of the features which distinguish it today. The red brick of the walls, which is now whitewashed, was then exposed. But Pearson did design some fittings for the church. The first of these was the oak Gothic pulpit. This was given in memory of Henry Cunliffe, who had been a generous subscriber to the building of St Barnabas but died a month after the church was completed. The square alabaster font supported on red marble columns dates from about the same time. But the oak choir stalls were not installed until 1893. Panelling round the walls of the apse followed nine years later. The most important feature of the church is the reredos. This takes the form of a carved wooden triptych, which was later gilded. The central panel displays the Crucifixion. The outer panels can be closed like doors. This reredos was designed by George Frederick Bodley, who was then in partnership with Thomas Garner. It was erected in 1907 and is a fine piece of work but rather too large for its site and impinges on the lancet windows of the apse. Bodley died during the year when it was erected. Thus Brighton and Hove have examples of his work from both ends of his career, from the church of St Michael and All Angels, Brighton, which was one of his earliest buildings, to this reredos, which was one of his latest works.

The stained-glass windows in St Barnabas are of various dates. The lancets in the polygonal chancel are by Clayton and Bell. The best window is at the west end and is a war memorial of the First World War. This was dedicated by the Bishop of Lewes in 1923. The artist seems not to be recorded. Below this window is a copy of the Last Supper by Leonardo da Vinci. This is thought to have been painted in the early nineteenth century and was bought in London in 1914 for £25 by the then vicar, the Rev. Francis Henry Dumville Smythe.

21

ALL SAINTS CHURCH, HOVE
(Hove parish church)

In 1878 the Rev. Walter Kelly retired from the united benefice of Hove-cum-Preston. In the following year the two parishes were separated by Order in Council, and the Rev. Thomas Peacey was appointed vicar of Hove itself. He had been educated at Clare College, Cambridge, where he was twenty-third wrangler, and ordained in 1869. In the short period between then and his arrival in Hove he had served as curate at St Margaret and St Nicholas's churches, King's Lynn (1869–73), St Anne's, Dublin (1873–4), Downton, near Salisbury (1874–6) and St Mark's, North Audley Street, London (1876–9).

Walter Kelly had built a vicarage for his own use, but as this was in Preston, Thomas Peacey's first priority was to build a vicarage for Hove parish. At that time the Stanford Estate was developing the land between Palmeira Square and Cliftonville which became the Avenues but was then known as West Brighton. Land for the purpose was obtained from the estate in what became Eaton Road between Wilbury Road and the Drive. This must have been purchased because the trustees of the Stanford Estate had previously offered a grant of land for a vicarage for St Barnabas's church, but the vice-chancellor had held that the trustees had no power to make a gift of the site. As architect of the vicarage Thomas Peacey chose John Loughborough Pearson, whose practice was largely ecclesiastical and amongst the most prolific of the nineteenth century. Construction of the vicarage began in 1883. The house is an L-shaped red-brick building in the style of the late fifteenth or early sixteenth century with trefoil-headed lights to the windows and a stone oriel on the first floor. Thomas Peacey had eleven children, so the house contained a large number of bedrooms, for which subsequent vicars of Hove have not blessed him.

It was from the first Thomas Peacey's intention to replace St Andrew's, Church Road, as the parish church by a more imposing building, and a design for it was even made by Pearson in 1880. But this had to wait for twelve years. However, the land for the church was acquired at the same time as for the vicarage, and it was intended that the church and vicarage, with its southern brick and flint wall, should form a group, designed by the same architect. The foundation stone of the church was laid on 25 April 1889.

Pearson was born in 1817. He designed St Augustine's, Kilburn, in 1871 and Truro cathedral in 1879. He was approaching the end of his life when All Saints was commissioned. In fact he died in 1897, before it was completed. If St Barnabas's, Hove had been one of his 'cheap editions', All Saints was a de luxe volume, and when Pearson was thinking in the grand manner he could outshine most other nineteenth-century church architects. All Saints is a fitting climax to his career.

The church is built of Sussex sandstone in thirteenth-century French Gothic style. It comprises a chancel with flanking chapels, a nave with aisles and a western narthex. Although not actually a cruciform building, it has a cruciform effect because the transeptal parts of the church are carried up higher than the aisles and chapels which adjoin them, to give the appearance of transepts. The nave and aisles took two years to build and were consecrated by the Bishop of Chichester, Dr Richard Durnford on 1 May 1891. The cost of this part of the building was £14,000, the builder John Shillitoe. The east end took another ten years. After Pearson's death in 1897 its construction was supervised by his son Frank Loughborough Pearson. This was consecrated by Dr Durnford's successor, Dr E. R. Wilberforce, on 1 November 1901. It was intended that the church should have a tower at its south-west angle, but only the base of this was built. At first-floor level in the south-west corner of the tower is a statue of the first vicar, the Rev. Thomas Peacey, carrying a model of the church. This lower portion of the tower and the narthex at the west end were not erected until 1924. The total cost was £40,000.

The church suffers from the usual defect of most Brighton and Hove churches in that it has a very restricted site and so can only be viewed to full effect from the south-west. It badly needs its missing tower which would have been a splendid object in its own right and would have uplifted the whole composition.

The real grandeur of the building resides in the interior. The arcades of

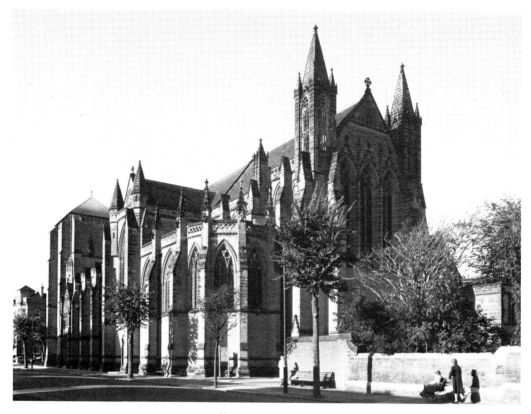

47 All Saints church, Hove

the nave are of cathedral proportions and quality. Part of the general effect is due to the fact that most of the important fittings were designed by Pearson himself, although some of them were carried out posthumously. The greatest of these is probably the reredos, which represents the Crucifixion. This was sculpted by Nathaniel Hitch, as were the five seats on the north wall of the chancel which are called the bishop's throne and the balancing sedilia on the south wall with their accompanying sculpture. These were all carried out by Frank Loughborough Pearson to his father's design and were not consecrated until 1908. The organ-case was built in 1915 to Frank Pearson's design and was given by A. M. Singer. The organ itself by William Hill & Son, had been inserted ten years earlier and is one of the finest instruments in the south of England. The choir stalls also date from 1915 and were the gift of a Mrs Ashley.

The chapel of the Holy Spirit to the south of the chancel is separated from the south 'transept' or aisle by a very fine wooden carved screen with a canopy

48 The interior of All Saints church, Hove

over it. This was a memorial to the parishioners who were killed in the First World War and was given by Major General and Colonel Marsland. The wrought-iron screen of the Jesus chapel on the north is a later insertion which was erected in memory of Canon Frederick James Meyrick, who was vicar of the church from 1929 to 1943. The pulpit is an octagonal stone one carved with biblical scenes. The baptistry in the north-west corner of the nave houses a font with an octagonal pink marble basin supported on green marble columns and topped by an octagonal wooden Gothic cover of three tiers.

The stained-glass windows were all designed by Clement Bell. The largest is the great west window, which was given by Major General Marsland in memory of King Edward VII, who as Prince of Wales had attended a service at the uncompleted church during a weekend visit to Reuben Sassoon at 7 Queen's Gardens in 1896. The window in the north 'transept' is a rose window, but the one with the most glowing colours is in the west corner of the south aisle. This dates from 1923.

In 1892, by Order in Council, All Saints became the parish church of Hove in the place of St Andrew's, Church Road. Thomas Peacey was made a canon of Chichester cathedral in 1891. He died in 1909 after a ministry of thirty years in Hove. His successor was the Rev. Leonard Hedley Burrows (1909–24). Only six incumbents have held the living since then. Bishop Horace Crotty, who was vicar from 1943 to 1952, was previously Bishop of Bath in Sydney, Australia, from 1928 to 1936.

22

UNION CHAPEL
(the Elim church)

The elements of a Non-conformist community existed in Brighthelmston after the Commonwealth, but the Conventicle Act of 1664 prevented them from manifesting themselves. Local Dissenters of all kinds had incurred the particular enmity of Captain Nicholas Tattersell. He had taken Charles II to France in 1651 after the battle of Worcester. At the Restoration he became a big man locally and when High Constable in 1670 took every step possible to suppress any dissenting communities that tried to show themselves.

It was not until the first year of the reign of William and Mary that a limited freedom of assembly was extended to Dissenters by the Toleration Act, 1689. On 15 March 1688/9 in return for £9 Edward Mighell conveyed to trustees a plot of land in Brighton on which to build a Presbyterian chapel. The site of this was in what is now known as Union Street, but was then only described as being in the Hempshares. A minister – the Rev. Ebenezer Bradshaw – materialised and remained on the scene until 1695, when he moved to Ramsgate. The community must have met at first in private houses or in a temporary building converted for the purpose, as no steps were taken to erect a permanent chapel until 1698–9. But incorporated in the present building is a stone with the date 1688 and the initials 'B.W.'. The first minister of the permanent building was the Rev. John Duke. He held the position from 1698 to 1745. New trustees were appointed in 1731, 1766, 1838 and 1844.

The community started life as a Presbyterian group. But during the ministry of John Duke it was agreed that presentation to the ministry should be alternately to a Presbyterian and an Independent representative. This arrangement gave rise to the chapel being called Union chapel. This name then caused the street to be called Union Street, and not the other way round.

By the time that the name of Union Street was well-established the chapel was henceforward more often known as Union Street chapel, but Union chapel is the older name. Incidently the adjoining street, Meeting House Lane, is also called after this chapel and not after the much later Friends' Meeting House.

The arrangement of alternate presentation lasted for about a hundred years. But at some time before 1838 Union chapel had become wholly an independent community. By 1800 a minister's house had been built adjoining Union chapel. The same year the chapel-yard was opened for burials. In 1810 during the ministry of the Rev. Dr John Styles (1808–23) the chapel was enlarged. From this period may date the present east front in Meeting House Lane. This is a traditional Sussex wall of cobbles with red-brick dressings and round-headed windows. These windows actually light a room on both storeys and not the chapel itself. In 1820 the gallery was removed and the apsidal space behind the pulpit converted into a vestry.

In 1824 a new minister was appointed who was to be one of the most important persons in the chapel's history. This was the Rev. John Nelson Goulty. He was born in Norfolk and was a kinsman of Admiral Lord Nelson. He came to Brighton from the Independent chapel at Henley-on-Thames. His ministry at Union chapel lasted thirty-seven years. Under his guidance the community quickly prospered. The debt of £1,000 was paid off, and in 1825 the congregation decided to rebuild the chapel. The design of the building is usually given to Amon Henry Wilds. But in that same year Charles Augustus Busby made a design for a chapel with a semi-circular interior, although the exterior differs from the chapel as built in having a portico of four columns. So Busby may have been responsible for the new building. The builder was named Field. The new building occupied the whole site, including the grave-yard and the minister's house. The new front along Union Street was in the fashionable Regency stuccoed manner with Doric pilasters and a pediment. But it was given a slight Egyptian feeling by the nature of the three large windows and two doorways, which are all wider at the bottom than at the top.

The entrance lobby on the south contains two elegant little staircases which lead to the gallery. The meeting house itself is dominated by this gallery. It forms a horseshoe or amphitheatre on three sides facing north and supported on eight cast iron columns with leaf capitals on the ground floor and Corinthian capitals above. The ceiling forms a half-dome of seven ribbed

49 Union chapel, Union Street 1853. Drawing by W. A. Delamotte

panels. The north wall has three blind round-headed arches. The pulpit, framed by the centre arch, originally took the form of a gallery set in a round-headed niche with a doorway below this that led to the staircase. The building seated 700 people. The work of building cost £1,110 and was completed in fifteen months. During the interregnum the congregation met in the Old Ship assembly rooms.

J. M. Goulty soon became a prominent man in Brighton. He lived first at 174 Western Road and later at 1 and 2 Sussex Square – a double house where his daughters also kept an academy for young ladies. From 1830 to 1832 he was honorary secretary of Sussex County Hospital. But education was his main interest. He founded the Brighton Union Charity School in Middle Street and was its honorary secretary from 1835 to 1866. Its first building was replaced by a more permanent structure in 1837. He was also one of the two honorary secretaries of the first Royal British School in

50 The original interior of Union chapel. Drawing by W. A. Delamotte

Edward Street, of which Lord John Russell laid the foundation stone in 1828. In 1847 Goulty established a preaching station at what was called the Bethel arch south of West Street. Goulty was an exact contemporary of the vicar of Brighton, the Rev. H. M. Wagner. They both came to Brighton in the same year (1824) and died in the same year (1870). At that time the relations of the Church of England and dissenting communities were bedevilled by the subject of compulsory church rates, to which Dissenters very naturally objected. This subject dominated Brighton Vestry meetings from 1836 until 1853. Wagner and Goulty were the principal protagonists in the matter and had many battles on the subject. In other respects they probably preserved good relations.

J. M. Goulty retired from the ministry at Union chapel in 1861 and died on 18 January 1870, aged 82. He was buried in the Extra Mural cemetery

51 The Rev. J. N. Goulty, minister of Union chapel 1824–70

in Brighton. He had a son named Horatio Nelson Goulty who was a fairly well-known architect. He designed the present Norfolk Hotel, King's Road, in 1865 to replace the older building on the site.

Alterations were made to the interior of Union chapel in 1875. The next minister of importance in the history of the building was the Rev. Reginald John Campbell. He was the son and grandson of a Congregational minister but went to Oxford with the intention of being ordained in the Church of England. However, he broke away from this. While still studying at Oxford he was approached by the temporary pastor at Union chapel during an interregnum there with an invitation signed by all the members of the congregation asking him to accept this Brighton ministry. Campbell there-fore accepted Congregational Orders instead of those of the Church of England and came to Union chapel in 1893. The chapel was then at rather a low ebb, but his preaching soon restored its fortunes to such a degree that four years later the building could not accommodate all those who wished to attend worship there.

There was in Brighton at that time one church which was on the same ecclesiological level as Union chapel. This was the Queen Square Congregational church. It had been built forty years earlier by a group of people in London who felt that there was a need for another Non-conformist church in the western part of Brighton. They first negotiated for a site in Cambridge Road, Hove, but this did not materialise. Instead they bought a plot of land for £1,600 on the east side of Queen Square. The money was advanced by Joshua Wilson and John Finch, both of Tunbridge Wells. They secured the assistance of the newly founded English Congregational Church Building Society. This was in fact the first church which the Society had sponsored. The foundation stone was laid by their treasurer, Rice Hopkins, on 3 October 1853. It was opened for worship on the 12 October 1854. The architects were James and Brown. It was a stone Gothic building in thirteenth-century style. It was intended to have a tower but this was never built. Beneath the church was a large undercroft for the Sunday school. The builder was John Fabian, and the cost £4,500. When completed, the building was conveyed to the English Congregational Chapel Building Society. They retained it until 1861, when it was made over to trustees on behalf of the congregation. The first minister was the Rev. John Leifchild.

At first the congregation only numbered about forty-seven. But by 1865 it was large enough to call for a bigger building. It was first proposed to demolish and rebuild completely. But this idea was rejected, and instead the chapel was enlarged at the north end by the addition of an apse in Decorated style. The interior was remodelled, and it was probably at this time that galleries with Gothic detail were added on the east, west and south sides. The architect of the alterations was named Poulton. The work cost £5,000.

By 1898 the chapel was somewhat in decline. It had an abundance of space, but a diminishing congregation. The Union Street chapel, on the other hand, had a constantly increasing congregation and insufficient space to accommodate them. It was therefore proposed that the two churches should merge. After much discussion this was agreed. Both ministers resigned, and a joint meeting of the two congregations invited the Rev. R. J. Campbell to be minister of the combined chapels under the name of Union church.

Campbell remained in office until 1903, when he received a call to the

City Temple church in London. His power as a preacher was such that the years from 1898 to 1903 were one of the two greatest periods in the history of Union church. The other such period was during the ministry of the Rev. Thomas Rhondda Williams from 1909 to 1931.

The Union Street chapel seems to have remained in use jointly with Union church during R. J. Campbell's ministry. But in 1905, after his departure, it was sold to the Glynn Vivian Miners Mission as a mission hall. This body had been founded by a rich industrialist named R. Glynn Vivian of Sketty Hall, Swansea, who owned copper works in Wales. In 1902 he suddenly went blind. When staying at the Metropole Hotel in Brighton after losing his sight he met a certain Colonel James Phillips, who converted him to Evangelism. He decided to devote some of his wealth to the improvement of the living conditions of miners throughout the world. The countries that he specifically named, besides Great Britain, were France, Germany, Spain, Russia, Siberia, South Africa and Chile. Having experienced his conversion to this work in Brighton he decided that the the headquarters of the foreign work should be in Brighton and so he bought Union Street chapel for the purpose. The mission occupied the building until 1931. It then reverted to use as a chapel and since that date has been occupied by the Elim Tabernacle or Free Church. The galleries remain in being, but no other original internal fittings survive.

23

THE FRIENDS' MEETING HOUSE

As in the case of the Presbyterians, a potential community of Friends existed in Brighton during the reign of Charles II, but the Conventicle Act of 1664 prevented their meeting in public. The Friends were not immune from the local persecution of all Dissenters that was organised by Captain Nicholas Tattersell and others. But they did manage to hold secret meetings in the then remote hamlet of West Blatchington.

When William and Mary came to the throne the Toleration Act, 1689, gave the Friends and other Dissenters a limited measure of freedom to meet in public. As a result, on 8 February 1690 a husbandman of Cowfold named Thomas Parsons conveyed to trustees for a hundred guineas an old malthouse on the north side of North Street for conversion into a 'decent meeting-house for the exercise of divine worship' It was an old building, having been erected as far back as 1637. It stood immediately to the west of what later came to be the Chapel Royal. With it went a narrow plot of land extending as far back as Church Street. This came to be known as the Quakers' Croft. Part of it was laid out as a burial-ground before 1734. New trustees were appointed in 1768.

About 1792 the piece of land adjoining the Quakers' Croft on the east became a pleasure ground or miniature Ranalagh known as the Promenade Grove. The exuberance of this did not accord with the sedate habits of the Friends, so about ten years later they decided to move their meeting house. It so happened that at that time the Prince of Wales was seeking to expand the grounds of his Brighton house in order to divert the line of Great East Street, as East Street was then called, which ran almost under the west windows of the Royal Pavilion. So in 1806 he bought the Quakers' Croft from the Friends for £800, apart from the meeting house itself which was

FRIENDS MEETING HOUSE.

52 The Friends' Meeting House 1853. Drawing by W. A. Delamotte

sold separately to William Verrall for £1,000. The building was then demolished and replaced by several shops.

To replace their old meeting house the Friends bought from John Glaisyer for £1,000 a plot of land on the east side of Ship Street with two cottages at the south-west corner of the site. The land was not then open to the road, as now, since that part of Prince Albert Street was not formed until thirty years later. The land was approached by a narrow passage between the cottages and 58 Ship Street. On this site the Friends built a new meeting house and caretaker's cottage adjoining on the south at the cost of £1,661. The builder was Richard Patching, whose firm of Patching & Son still exists today. It was first opened for worship in 1805. It was a simple pedimented red-brick building of two storeys with round-headed windows and, on the ground floor, Venetian shutters. The entrance was then on the north side by means of a wide portico. Adjoining on the south was a cottage for the caretaker of three storeys with segmental-headed windows. The only internal decoration of the meeting house was a wide coved sounding-board over the speakers' end of the room and a gallery at the west end. About 400 people

PULL THIS SHUTTER DOWN FIRST.

53 The interior of the Friends' Meeting House 1853. Drawing by W. A. Delamotte

could be seated. Part of the land was laid out as a grave-yard, and the cottages at the south-west corner were let.

In 1838 the new road which constitutes that part of Prince Albert Street was constructed by Isaac Bass, who had purchased and demolished the old vicarage in Nile Street adjoining. He was himself a member of the Society of Friends. The Friends gave up a portion of their grave-yard, and the two cottages in Ship Street were demolished. Further burials in the grave-yard were prohibited in March 1854 by an Order in Council made under the Burial of the Dead beyond the Metropolis Act, 1853. To replace their burial-ground the Friends therefore obtained a plot of land at Black Rock which was then in the parish of Rottingdean, but later became Riflebutt Road. This was the gift of Charles Beard of the Elms, Rottingdean, who owned most of the land in that parish and was a member of the Rottingdean Quakers' meeting. This plot was walled in, turfed and opened for burials in 1855.

54 The Friends' Meeting House 1987

It was in its turn obliterated by the road approaches to the Brighton Marina when these were built in the 1970s.

In 1876 the Society of Friends decided to add an educational institute to the meeting house. This took the form of an L-wing in matching style to the north-east of the original building. It contained a large lecture-room with classrooms over. The architects were Clayton & Holford, who subsequently became Clayton & Black. The building was opened on 24 January 1877. At the same time the portico of the meeting house was moved from the west to the north side. The interior was remodelled and the gallery made narrower. This slightly reduced the seating accommodation.

After the Second World War the institute became the Friends centre, an adult education centre supported financially by the Friends, by the local authorities and by private bodies. This is today one of the most active cultural organisations in the town.

171

24

THE UNITARIAN CHURCH

The early history of the Unitarian church in Brighton is interwoven with that of the Baptist community. In 1791 William Stevens came to the town and found that a group of Calvinist Baptists met in New Street, as Bond Street was then called. Their pastor was Thomas Vine. Stevens was much influenced by the preaching of the Rev. Elhanan Winchester of South Place chapel, Finsbury, which eventually became the South Place Ethical Society. Winchester was an American Baptist minister who had adopted Universalist views. Stevens introduced these views into the Brighton group, with the result that nineteen of the members, including Stevens and Thomas Vine, were expelled from the congregation on 13 October 1795 for no longer believing in eternal damnation. The dissenting band met elsewhere for a short period but was soon scattered. William Stevens, however, decided to hold services in his own house. The first of these took place on 7 May 1797. The only people present were Stevens's own family and four friends. But they soon joined with fourteen members of the General Baptist Society of Worship Street, London, whose preacher was a layman called Gillam. After four years the joint congregation numbered about fifty. This was too large for a private house, so in 1806 they rented a small chapel in Jew Street, which was part of Bond Street. Ministers from Lewes, Southover and Ditchling came over to help with the services.

When a Unitarian missionary named Richard Wright preached at the chapel Gillam and some other members of the congregation embraced the ideas of Unitarianism. Through some misunderstanding Gillam resigned the position of preacher, and William Stevens became the leader of the community. But the congregation was then diminishing. It was rescued from further decline by John Chatfield, the leader of the Unitarian community in Ditchling. He secured the help of the British and Foreign Unitarian Society, which gave financial assistance. The chapel in Jew Street was closed, and another meeting-room acquired in Cavendish Street. This was later known as the Biblical Lecture Rooms. The room was opened for worship in July 1812. The first preacher was the Rev. Robert Aspland from London, but the leader of the community remained William Stevens. Services were held there for eight years.

In March 1819 John Chatfield purchased for £650 a plot of land on the west side of New Road, which was then being developed after being given to the town by the Prince Regent. An appeal was made for the purpose of building a new chapel. Chatfield gave £200 in addition to the gift of the site. Someone called Holden gave a similar sum. The building was opened for worship on 20 August 1820. The architect was Amon Henry Wilds, who was just then beginning his career in Brighton. The first minister was Dr Morell. He held the view that a modern church should be designed on the lines of a classical Greek temple. So the new Unitarian church was modelled on the Thesaeum in Athens. It is one of three buildings with this derivation that were designed by this architect. The second of these was the original St Mary's church, Rock Gardens (1827), and the third was the Town Hall in the High Street at Gravesend (1836).

The entrance of the Unitarian Church is stuccoed and forms a grand portico of four giant fluted Doric columns with a pediment over. Originally the frieze contained the words in Greek letters: 'To God only wise be glory through Jesus Christ'. But these words were removed by a later minister on the grounds that they would be misunderstood by the general public. The forecourt was originally enclosed by an elegant iron railing with brick piers, but this was removed in 1929. The humbler north and south sides of the church, which are hardly seen, are faced with brown brick with tall round-headed windows.

The central doorway leads into a lobby which originally contained a large alms dish in the form of a terracotta vase. The main interior was at first absolutely plain. There was a deep cove to the central flat of the ceiling. The tall round-headed windows were lit with plain glass. There were box-pews but no galleries. The only feature was the pulpit in the centre of the west wall. This was raised on a supporting column and flanked by a pair of desks and doorways leading to the vestry and the schoolroom. The church seated 350.

55 The Unitarian church, New Road

The first minister, Dr Morell, remained in office for seven years. He was succeeded in 1829 by the Rev. J. P. Malleson, who also ran a school in Hove. He remained minister until his retirement in 1860. The congregation at that time numbered between 100 and 150. The next minister was the Rev. Robert Ainslie, who had been a Congregational minister. During his ministry the church was modernised. A new pulpit with an iron-work front was installed and behind it a panelled reredos of the Ten Commandments and the Beatitudes. A gallery was built at the east end which contained the organ. The church at this time was known as the Unsectarian church. Robert Ainslie attracted a large congregation, but in 1874 he was forced by ill health to retire. £276 was subscribed by the congregation as a parting gift to him.

Following his resignation attendances fell. A committee was formed to carry on the church. Eventually in 1875 the Rev. T. R. Dobson, who also had been a Congregational minister, was chosen as the next minister. He

174

56 The interior of the Unitarian church *c.* 1950

removed the Greek lettering from the frieze of the portico and renamed the
church the Free Christian church. He also built a larger Sunday school or
lecture hall (now called the Unitarian church hall) to the south-west of the
church. This cost £600. Ainslie remained in office till 1886.

The name of the church has been altered slightly several times since 1875.
In 1901 it was called the Free Christian church (Christ church), in 1922 the
Free Christian church (Unitarian) and in 1932 Christ church (Unitarian). In
recent years it has generally been known just as the Unitarian church.

In the late nineteenth century stained glass was inserted in one of the
windows as the gift of Ellen Elizabeth Nye Chart, who was the proprietress
and manager of the adjoining Theatre Royal in New Road from 1876 till
1892. Alterations to the interior of the church were carried out in 1938 and
more substantially in 1966. On one of these occasions, probably in 1966,
the box-pews were removed and replaced by chairs, except for the benches
along the north and south walls. The east gallery has been underbuilt to provide a vestry and a committee room. A curtain has taken the place of the

pulpit as the central western feature. Today the most prominent feature comprises the handsome pair of Regency-style doorcases that flank this curtain. These tall openings with their garland friezes are a great improvement on the simple doorways shown in the drawing by W. A. Delamotte of the interior of the church in 1858.

25

THE HANOVER CHAPEL

(the Brighton Presbyterian church)

The first meeting-place of the Presbyterian community in Brighthelmston was in what is now called Union Street but was then only known as the Hempshares. This was established there from 1698 onwards for over a hundred years. In the eighteenth century the chapel was partly Independent, but the Presbyterian connection was not finally severed until the early years of the nineteenth century at some time before 1838. In 1825 Stephen Wood of Lindfield, who had already built Independent chapels in Lindfield and Cuckfield, erected an Independent chapel between Church Street and North Road in Brighton which was called the Hanover chapel. It cost £4,000 and seated 1,200 people. It may well have been designed by Amon Wilds and/or Charles Augustus Busby, the partnership which was responsible for so many of the best buildings to be erected in Brighton during the 1820s.

The main front faces south across the grave-yard and is a balanced architectural composition of two storeys, faced with stucco. The end window bays, flanked by Doric pilasters, project slightly and are surmounted by small pediments. Their chief feature is a pair of Doric porches with solid parapets. The parapet between the end pediments has a raised central panel topped by acroteriae. On the ground floor are two round-headed windows set in Doric half-columns. The interior had galleries on three sides, the south end being curved, and box-pews. The principal feature was a two-decker pulpit in the centre of the north wall.

The chapel and burial-ground to the south were vested in trustees. Stephen Wood nominated his son-in-law, the Rev. James Edwards of Petworth as the first minister. Edwards lived in a house in Windsor Terrace opposite the chapel. He was not a good preacher, and eventually the attendance at the chapel declined. In 1843 he appointed the Rev. Frederick Allin of Homerton

57 The Hanover chapel, Church Street (Presbyterian church) *c.* 1960

College as his assistant. Allin was only twenty-four and evidently had the gifts which Edwards lacked, so the chapel was again filled. But Allin complicated matters by falling in love with Edwards's daughter. As he was not accepted as a suitor, the couple eloped. On returning to Brighton Allin held services in the Old Ship assembly rooms, which drew many of the congregation away from the Hanover chapel.

Edwards was so discouraged by these events that on 6 May 1846 he leased the chapel for ninety-nine years at a rent of £60 a year to a group of people in Lewes who were of the Presbyterian persuasion. He himself became a Presbyterian minister elsewhere. The Hanover chapel was opened for Presbyterian services on 2 October 1847. The first Presbyterian minister was the Rev. Alexander J. Ross. But in 1852 he was deposed for heresy and later entered the ministry of the Church of England.

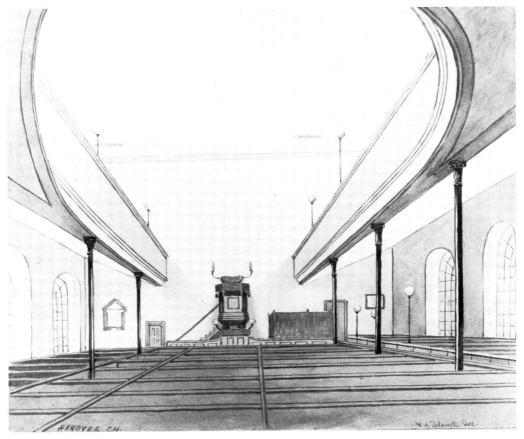

58 The original interior of the Hanover chapel, Church Street. Drawing by W. A. Delamotte

In March 1854 further use of the grave-yard was prohibited by Order in Council made under the Burial of the Dead beyond the Metropolis Act, 1853. Eight years later the freehold of the chapel was purchased by the community for £2,184. 11s. 10d. This included three schoolrooms, the land of the burial-ground and two cottages at the south end of this, adjoining Church Street. In 1863 a parish hall was erected on the north side of the chapel at the cost of £30. This has been demolished since 1980. During the ministry of the Rev. Alexander B. Mackay (1872–9) the original pulpit was replaced by a platform pulpit and the box-pews were removed. Pew rents were abolished. The name of the chapel was changed to the Queen's Road Presbyterian church, but it came to be better known as the Brighton Presbyterian church. It is now called the Brighthelm church. The interior has been gutted over the years and now retains none of its original fittings.

179

When the Presbyterian and Congregational Churches amalgamated nationally as the United Reformed Church in 1972 the Hanover chapel was linked with Union church in Queen's Square, as Union church had previously been with the Union Street chapel. Union church was the more vigorous ecclesiastical community of the two, but as the Presbyterian church was a listed building it was decided to retain the latter as the place of worship for both communities and to add to it a large community centre for social work. Union church has been demolished, and the site sold to finance the project. The Presbyterian church was also closed in 1972 and is part of the new Brighthelm Church Centre.

26

L'EGLISE FRANÇAISE REFORMÉE

This little church is a rarity. There are only two other French Protestant congregations in England. One meets in the crypt of Canterbury cathedral. The other has its own church in Soho Square, London. The French church in Brighton is also very little known and is almost a secret place. It is now surrounded and dwarfed by the Hotel Metropole on the south and by the latter's exhibition halls and by Sussex Heights on the north. The church is only accessible from Queensbury Mews leading off King's Road and from Preston Street.

The community likes to think that its origins and traditions go back to 1548. In that year a French-speaking refugee from Dilsen near Liège in Flanders, who was a practising Calvinist, came to Brighton to escape the persecution of his faith by the Spanish government which then ruled his country. His name was Deryck Carver. He was a brewer by trade and established a brewery in Black Lion Street on the site occupied by the public house which now bears his name. The building which subsisted there until 1974 dated largely from the eighteenth century and was built of cobbles with red-brick dressings. But the ground floor of the north wall along Black Lion Lane was certainly older than the eighteenth century and might have gone back to Carver's time. When the building was reconstituted and rebuilt as a replica in 1974 this older wall was to have been preserved and reincorporated in the new building. But by an unfortunate misunderstanding it was demolished and the materials reused in a new wall. So this interesting possible link with Deryck Carver has been lost. But the cellars of the old Black Lion, which was renamed at the time of the rebuilding the 'Deryck Carver', may go back to Carver's time. His association with the site is also commemorated by a stone tablet, which was erected on the older building in the 1920s and replaced in 1974. The eighteenth-century weather-vane in the form of a black lion has also been preserved. It was restored by the Regency Society of Brighton and Hove in 1974 and re-erected on the new building.

Deryck Carver was a 'predicant' or lay reader in the Calvinist church, although it is doubtful whether he could read at the time when he lived in Brighton. He probably learned to do so during his later imprisonment in London. He held bible readings at his house in Brighton. These were attended by the fishermen from both sides of the English Channel who spoke French. When Queen Mary came to the throne in 1553 and Roman Catholicism became again the official religion such meetings were prescribed. But Carver continued to hold his bible readings, so he was arrested and sent to London for imprisonment and trial. He was subsequently burned at the stake at Lewes on 22 July 1555. A number of other Protestant martyrs suffered the same fate at Lewes during Queen Mary's reign and are commemorated by an obelisk on the western slope of Cliffe Hill there.

During the next 130 years the Church of England became the established religion of the country but did not extend freedom of worship to Non-conformists. The people who practised Calvinism were obliged to continue meeting secretly in private houses until the Toleration Act, 1689, gave them a little freedom. A Presbyterian or Independent chapel was built in 1698–9 in what is now Union Street to provide for their worship. French-speaking people attended meetings at this chapel during the next 150 years, and its registers contain many French names.

In about 1858 it was thought that French-speaking people were sufficiently numerous in Brighton to justify forming a congregation of their own, and a pastor named the Rev. Caesar Pascal was summoned from Nîmes to minister to them. Three years later he was succeeded by the Rev. A. Gonin, who remained in office for twenty-one years. The first services were held at 18 Montpelier Villas in the house of an English lady named Mrs E. Hayes, whose husband was a clergyman. A committee was formed of which the Rev. Dr J. G. Gregory, the minister of Emmanuel church, Norfolk Terrace, was chairman. The honorary secretary was the Rev. E. L. Roxby, who was perpetual curate of St Margaret's church. Both churches had always had Evangelical leanings in sympathy with Non-conformism. This committee was later replaced by a church council, of which most of the members were English but which was assisted by an auxiliary committee, the majority of whose members were French.

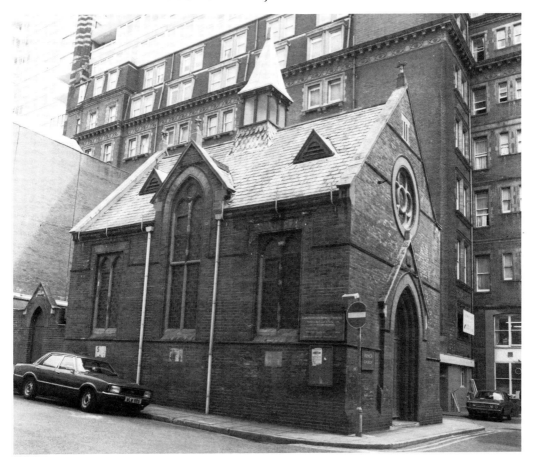

59 L'Eglise Française Reformée, Queensbury Mews

From 1860 onwards the services were held in public buildings. This was at first in the Queen's Road Presbyterian church. The community later met at the Royal Newburgh assembly rooms in St Margaret's Place. When this closed they tried to buy the building for £3,000 but were unsuccessful in doing so. They therefore had to revert to the Queen's Road Presbyterian church or to St Margaret's church hall. After a spell at the Union Street chapel they met at a building in Cannon Place which no longer exists but was then called 'Little Vic'.

Eventually it was decided that the community should build its own church. Pastor Gonin made a tour of Protestant communities in France to raise the money to buy a site in Queensbury Mews behind King's Road. The Metropole Hotel did not exist at that time. Substantial sums were given by Mrs Hayes, her brother John Lawrence and her friends, Mademoiselle Abrassard and Mademoiselle Petitory. The balance was raised by the congregation. The foundation stone was laid by Mrs Hayes on 18 July 1887. The architect was J. G. Gibbins and the contractor W. D. B. Field. The site cost £735 and the building about £800.

The church is a very small red-brick building in rudimentary Gothic style with windows comprising pairs of pointed lancets in the exposed west front. The south or entrance front has a tall pointed archway surmounted by a pediment with a terracotta relief (now much worn) of the Bible in the tympanum. Above the slate roof is a small square glazed turret with a copper spirelet. Dr Gregory presided at the inauguration of the church in March 1888 in the presence of the mayor of Brighton.

At the turn of the century the French-speaking colony in Brighton probably numbered as many as 2,000. Many of them were of the Protestant faith, and the congregation at the Reformed church was fairly large. The best known pastor was probably the Rev. Honoré Migot, who served there from 1921 until his death in 1947. Since that time the congregation has dwindled, and there is no longer a resident pastor.

27

THE ROMAN CATHOLIC CHURCH OF ST JOHN THE BAPTIST

The penal laws against Roman Catholics lasted a hundred years longer than those against Dissenters. In 1778 and 1791 Catholic Relief Acts at last introduced a measure of toleration for Catholics. The second of these Acts made it lawful for Catholic churches to be built, provided that these did not have a bell or steeple, in other words provided they did not look like churches. Nine hundred Roman Catholic churches were built between 1791 and 1841. One of the first of these was in Brighthelmston. The resident Catholic community there at the end of the eighteenth century must have been very small, but it was considerably augmented after 1790 by refugees from the French revolution. The significance of the community was also emphasised by the residence in Brighton of Maria Fitzherbert.

On 15 December 1785 Mrs Fitzherbert had gone through a form of marriage according to the rites of the Church of England with George, Prince of Wales, although the ceremony was not only invalid but actually illegal. When the Prince made his regular visits to Brighton Mrs Fitzherbert accompanied him, but she never slept at the Royal Pavilion. She always had her own house in the town. The site of her first house is not known, but it probably was at the north-east end of Great East Street, as East Street was then called. Robert Adam made a plan for a house for her in Brighton, but it is not certain whether this was ever built. Later, in 1804, William Porden, the architect of the Dome, designed for her a house in the Old Steine. This building (Steine House, 54 Old Steine) is still standing, although it was disastrously refronted eighty years later. Mrs Fitzherbert herself may not have played any active part in the establishment of the first Roman Catholic church in Brighton as the period when it was first mooted coincided with the years when she was estranged from the Prince under the influence of Lady Jersey.

However, she lived to play such an important role in the history of the Roman Catholic community in Brighton that she can almost be considered as their patron saint.

In 1798 a Catholic mission was established in Brighton over a boat shop in Margaret Street. The man largely responsible for its foundation was the Rev. Philip Wyndham, who was chaplain to successive Dukes of Norfolk at Arundel. The first missionary rector was the Rev. William Barnes. His successor in 1804 was a French émigré priest, the Rev. Joseph Mouchel. The accommodation in Margaret Street having proved unsatisfactory, other temporary premises were tried in Castle Square, Prospect Row and North Street successively. But in 1805 Joseph Mouchel joined forces with a certain Dr Collins to raise money to build a permanent church. They found a site for a church and a presbytery on the east side of High Street, where 47 and 48 High Street now stand. The building was erected in 1806–7. The west front facing the street had a simple classical façade with three large round-headed windows at first-floor level and a parapet over. The interior was very plain and in fact not much different from that of a Protestant preaching box of the period. Fashion seems to play a very important part in the church arrangements of all periods, as can be seen in the re-ordering of modern churches, both Protestant and Catholic alike, to provide detached altars. The new Brighton Catholic church had two fireplaces on one of the long walls and a gallery at the west end. It is a pity that we have no record of whether or not the pulpit was of the elaborate design which characterised contemporary Protestant churches. The presbytery stood on the south side of the church.

In 1818 the Rev. Edward Cullin became missionary rector. He was a friend of Mrs Fitzherbert's and was to lead the Catholic community in Brighton during the next thirty-two years until his death in 1850. He immediately made plans to enlarge the church. Mrs Fitzherbert gave £1,000 for the purpose. The passing of Catholic emancipation in 1829 enabled the community to set their sights wider. An appeal was launched to build a larger church elsewhere. £6,000 was raised. Mrs Fitzherbert may possibly have given another £1,000, but this is not certain. Another benefactor was Isaac Cooper of County Wicklow.

The trustees were able to purchase a site in East Brighton from the Marquess of Bristol for £1,050. This was to the east of Upper St James's Street on open land which later came to be the junction of Upper Bedford Street and Bedford Road. The new church was built by William Hallett, who was a prominent Brighton citizen and later became the second mayor of the town from 1855–6. He seems also to have acted as architect, although he is not known to have designed any other buildings.

The new church of St John the Baptist is a plain stuccoed building in classical style. For the principal or southern elevation all that Hallett did was to produce more or less a replica of the main front of St Mary's Roman Catholic church, Moorfields in London. This may have been on instructions from his employers as St Mary's was at that time the headquarters of the Roman Catholic Church in England. If so, this may account for the community having given the commission to a builder, rather than to an architect who would have produced an original design. Both churches have recessed porches with giant Corinthian columns and a pediment over the whole façade. Only the arrangement of doorways and windows differs. St John's has side entrances in the porch, which flank the central doorway, and blind doorways in the flanking bays of the front with windows over these. The forecourt was originally enclosed by iron railings, but these were taken for salvage during the Second World War. Like so many Anglican churches in Brighton, the building was orientated north to south. The interior was quite plain, as the church in High Street had been. The main feature was a shallow sanctuary recess flanked by Corinthian columns. This framed a bas-relief over the altar of the baptism of Christ by St John the Baptist. This altar-piece was carved by John Edward Carew. There was a gallery at the south end of the church. A presbytery was built to the west of the church.

St John's was consecrated by Bishop Branston, the Vicar Apostolic of the London District, on 7 July 1835 and opened for public worship two days later. Although many Roman Catholic churches had been opened since the Catholic Relief Act, 1791, this was only the fourth Catholic church to be consecrated since the Reformation. The old church in High Street was sold. It was subsequently used for a variety of commercial purposes and finally demolished in 1981.

Mrs Fitzherbert died at her Brighton house on 27 March 1837. She was buried nine days later in a vault under St John's church. The emplacement of the coffin was marked a hundred years later by a stone placed immediately above it in the floor of the church in the centre of the main aisle. A memorial to her, sculpted by John Edward Carew, was erected in the south-east corner of the nave. It shows her kneeling figure with the left hand outstretched. On this were placed three wedding rings for her marriages to Edward Weld,

60 The original interior of St John the Baptist's Roman Catholic church. Drawing by
W. A. Delamotte

Thomas Fitzherbert and George IV as Prince of Wales. The monument was
cleaned and regilded in 1963 by the Regency Society of Brighton and Hove.

Edward Cullin, Mrs Fitzherbert's friend who was the first missionary rector of the church died on 5 March 1850. A memorial to him, probably also
by John Edward Carew, was placed on the west wall of the nave. Before
Edward Cullin's death the Rev. Henry Rymer had been appointed as his
assistant. In 1869 Canon Rymer, as by then he had become, was appointed
rector and remained in office until his death in 1887.

In 1854 a school was started to the north-west of the Presbytery. Four
years later the Sisters of Mercy, who had established a convent in Egremont
Place, moved to Bedford Lodge to the east of St John's church. A west wing
was added to this in 1866 to connect the convent with the church. The con-

61 Maria Fitzherbert's tomb in St John the Baptist's Roman Catholic church

62 St John the Baptist's Roman Catholic church 1987

vent chapel followed in 1874. During this period the Roman Catholic community in Brighton greatly increased in size. A second Catholic church was built in 1860–2. This was St Mary Magdalene's, Upper North Street, which was designed by Gilbert Robert Blount.

At the same time it was felt that St John's needed enlargement, so in 1866 land to the north of the church was purchased for £1,100. However, no steps were taken to build on it until the early 1870s. Then the same architect, G. R. Blount, was commissioned to replace the sanctuary recess by a proper chancel with a barrel-vaulted roof and flanking chapels separated by Corinthian columns and gilded capitals. The chapels were dedicated to the Sacred Heart and the Virgin Mary respectively. Carew's altar-piece was moved to the baptistry at the south-east end of the nave. The builders were Patching & Weller. The new building cost £2,000 and was consecrated in 1875. During 1879 Cardinal Newman attended mass at the church while visiting his sisters in Brighton and preached his first sermon there after being appointed a Cardinal. This was not his first connection with the town as, during his Anglican days, he had frequently visited his mother in Marine Square.

In 1887 Father Johnston, who had been assistant priest since 1876, became missionary rector and held the position until his death in 1916. His first act as rector was to commission S. J. Nicholl to design a grander church in Byzantine style. But this scheme was never carried out. Instead, as the fashion for plain interiors in both Anglo-Catholic and Roman Catholic churches had passed, Nathaniel Hubert Westlake was given the job of decorating the whole church with mural paintings. These took him several years to execute and cost £540. As murals, they are not distinguished but they do furnish what would otherwise be a rather bare interior. They were restored in 1957 for greater expenditure than the original cost. A certain number of other alterations were made in the same period, of which the most important was probably the introduction from a Belgian church of very handsome seventeenth-century Baroque altar rails.

Since that date the only alteration of significance which the church has sustained has been the addition in 1976 of a porch at the south-west corner with a ramped approach outside it. This has become the main entrance of the church.

28

THE SYNAGOGUE

There was a small Jewish community in Brighton by the end of the eighteenth century. Its founder was Emanuel Hyam Cohen, who had emigrated from Niederwerren in Bavaria and settled in Brighton in 1782. He kept a school in Artillery Place (the site of the Grand Hotel) and died in 1823. The first synagogue was in existence as early as 1792 and was in Jew Street, which was part of New Street, as Bond Street was then called. It is said to have contained fifty seats, but there was no gallery for women. By 1808 the synagogue had moved to the east side of West Street towards the south end. It was approached down an alley named Pounes Court – one of those small courtyards of cottages which were a special feature of the original streets of Brighton before the middle of the nineteenth century. It is likely that the building was no more than a room in the house of a Jewish family. The rabbi was named Cohen.

The 1820s, however, saw the establishment of a more substantial religious building. In 1823 the congregation took a lease for ninety-nine years from William Gilburd of the New Steine Hotel, New Steine, of a plot of land on the east side of Devonshire Place. On this they erected a synagogue, of which the façade is still in existence. The builder was Benjamin Bennett. The street elevation is a simple Regency stuccoed front with Doric pilasters and a pediment. In the latter, the words 'Jews Synagogue 5598' can still just be deciphered. The building again held fifty people but this time had a ladies' gallery.

As early as 1824 it was proposed to raise the sum of £300 needed to purchase the freehold of the building. But it was not until 1836 that the land was actually conveyed to trustees on behalf of the congregation. David Mocatta, who later designed Brighton station, was then commissioned to

63 The interior of the old Synagogue in Devonshire Place. Drawing by W. A. Delamotte

enlarge the building. In addition to the synagogue itself the new building comprised a residence for the minister, schoolrooms and a workshop of two storeys. The latter was probably a unique feature of any synagogue in England. The Jewish community continued to use the building until 1875. Drawings by W. A. Delamotte, made in 1853, exist of both the exterior and the interior. The latter shows the central bimah or enclosed space.

By 1860 the local community only amounted to about forty families, but there were so many visitors to Brighton that the synagogue was sometimes not large enough to accommodate all who attended. It was, however, not until 1874 that a new site was obtained on the east side of Middle Street (no. 66). The foundation stone of a new building was laid by Louis Cohen of London on 19 November 1874 in the presence of the chief rabbi, Dr Nathan Adler, and the mayor of Brighton, Alderman J. L. Brigden. When it was completed the old synagogue (37 Devonshire Place) was sold subject to restrictive covenants that it should not be used as another place of worship or as a public house or music hall. It actually became a sale room and is today occupied by the Health Sharpe Studios.

The architect of the new building in Middle Street was Thomas Lainson, who was architect to the Goldsmid and the Vallence estates at Hove and designed the Cliftonville Congregational church, Ventnor Villas, Hove. The builders were Cheesman & Sons. The synagogue took just under a year to build and cost £12,000. Louis Cohen, who laid the foundation stone, gave £200. Much of the money was raised by Lewis Lewis, the grandson of Hyam Lewis. The latter was a jeweller and pawnbroker who was probably the most prominent member of the Jewish community in Brighton from 1816 until 1851. The building is of white brick with variegated brick relieving arches and red marble shafts to the columns of the windows and doorway but stone bases and capitals. It is in Byzantine style, somewhat similar to that of the Bayswater synagogue. The principal elevation facing west has a recessed centre and projecting wings, surmounted by a pediment containing a rose window and the inscription 'How tremendous is this place! This is none other than the house of God.' The building strikes a restrained note which does not stand out from the muted atmosphere that now characterises Middle Street since the tide of residence has departed. Behind the synagogue on the east were built a house for the minister and, as in Devonshire Place, school-rooms of two storeys for about twenty-five children. These subsidiary buildings still exist, but the ground floor of the minister's house has been converted into meeting rooms, and the first floor is now the caretaker's flat. The land was conveyed to a council of nine representatives and two wardens. The synagogue was dedicated on the 23 September 1875 by the chief rabbi, Dr Nathan Adler, who subsequently came to live in Hove. It seated 300 people. A banquet was held the same evening in the Royal Pavilion, which was presided over by Sir David Lionel Salomans. The first minister was the Rev. A. C. Jacobs.

Nothing about the exterior prepares one for the splendour of the inside. This is certainly, after the Royal Pavilion, the most spectacular interior in Brighton. But it was not so in 1875. All the remarkable fittings were given individually during the years from 1875 to 1914 by prominent members of the congregation, usually in memory of members of their family. Most numerous amongst them are gifts of the Sassoon family, several members

64 The interior of the present Synagogue in Middle Street

of which had houses in Brighton and Hove during that period. These gifts are all recorded in stone tablets on the west wall of the west vestibule.

The main hall has galleries on the north, south and west sides with red marble columns and foliated brass capitals. These enclose round-headed arches at the upper level, behind which each gallery has half a barrel-vaulted ceiling. The pews in and below the galleries are now enclosed by elaborate and very beautiful iron railings, finished with brass tops and finials. The

195

central bimah or enclosed space with the warden's seat to the east of it is similarly surrounded by equally beautiful railings and surmounted by lamp standards with shades in imitation of flames. In front of this is a brass and black marble portable candelabrum or chaukia, which dates from about 1845 and was brought from the old synagogue in Devonshire Place.

The stained-glass windows are all of floral design and of matching style throughout the building. They were individual gifts, many of them from the Sassoon family. Two windows towards the east end were presented in memory of Lady Rosebery. She was born Hannah Rothschild, daughter of Baron de Rothschild of Mentmore in Buckinghamshire. Her husband went on to be Prime Minister after her death.

The most spectacular part of the building is the sanctuary at the east end. This is enclosed by another very fine railing. The east end forms an apse with canted panels of mosaic surmounted by elaborate plasterwork and three stained-glass windows above. Behind the western railing is a magnificent brass lectern. This was given in 1887 by Sir Albert Sassoon of 1 Eastern Terrace, Brighton, on the occasion of the marriage of his son, Edward, afterwards the second baronet, to Aline Rothschild of the Paris branch of that family. This lectern is flanked by splendid brass candelabra which were the gift of Baroness Mayer de Rothschild, the mother of Lady Rosebery. But perhaps the most beautiful item in the synagogue comprises the brass gates and overthrow of the Ark. Originally in 1875 the Ark had rosewood shutters. These were replaced by the present gates in 1905. They were the gift of David Reuben Sassoon and his sisters in memory of their parents, Reuben David and Catherine Sassoon. This branch of the family lived at 7 Queen's Gardens, Hove.

All these marvellous fittings in the Brighton synagogue make its interior probably the finest of any synagogue in England and amongst the most splendid in Europe.

29

ST PETER'S CHURCH, PRESTON
(Preston old parish church)

The first outlying village to be absorbed into the Borough of Brighton was Preston, in 1868. The nucleus of the old village is still to be seen to the west of the London Road in North Road, Middle Road and South Road. The manor house, which was originally called Preston House and later Preston Place, stands slightly to the south-east, on the other side of the main road. It is now a museum or a furnished country house which was given to Brighton Council by Sir Charles and Lady Thomas Stanford during their lives and passed into the Council's ownership on their deaths in 1932. The original parish church of St Peter's nestles in the trees immediately to the east of the manor house.

There was a church here at the time of the Domesday survey, but it was rebuilt in the thirteenth century, probably in about 1260. It comprises a chancel, nave and west tower. The north porch of today and the balancing vestry to the south are modern additions. The tower is unusually small in proportion to the remainder of the building. It actually stands in the garden of the manor house because in 1547 Richard Elrington was allowed by the vicar and inhabitants of Preston to take part of the church-yard into his garden provided that he built two walls running south to north from the west end of the church. The tower has a pyramidical tiled cap.

The altar is the altar-tomb of Richard Elrington, who held the manor and died in 1515. He was the father of the Richard Elrington who enclosed part of the church-yard in 1547. The wooden reredos above it dates from 1906, when it replaced a painting of the removal of Christ's body from the Cross which now hangs over the south doorway of the nave. This picture is attributed to Sir Edward Burne-Jones. The medieval triple sedilia and piscina in the chancel have been so much restored in the nineteenth century that

65 St Peter's church, Preston

they have largely the character of that date. The piscina in the south–east corner of the nave is more genuine. The font, adjoining it, has a Saxon bowl which was discovered in the grounds of Preston manor.

The chief feature of the interior comprises the thirteenth-century wall-paintings. These were plastered over at the Reformation and were only redis-covered in 1830. The north wall shows the Last Supper, which is separated by a strip or frieze of clouds from a narrow scene of the Nativity below. On each side of the chancel arch are the martyrdom of St Thomas of Canter-bury and St Michael weighing souls. The interior of the church suffered a bad fire in 1906, when the frescoes were much damaged. But when volume 7 of the *Victoria County History for Sussex* appeared in 1940, and the Sussex volume of Pevsner's *The Building of England* was published twenty-five years later, further scenes could still be seen over the chancel arch, representing the incredulity of St Thomas, Saints Catherine and Margaret, a bishop (pos-sibly St Nicholas) and a woman. But these are no longer visible.

On the north wall of the chancel there was once a mural tablet to the memory of Anthony Shirley, his wife and twelve children, but this has disappeared. The Shirley family was widely dispersed throughout Sussex. They inherited Preston manor from the Elringtons by marriage and owned it from 1569 to 1705. The house then passed, again by marriage, to the Westerns, who have no memorial in the church. In 1794 Thomas Western sold the house to William Stanford, whose father, Richard Stanford, had been a tenant of the manor since at least 1758. The chancel of the church contains many memorials to the Stanford family, although their graves are at West Dean near Chichester. In the south wall is a window in memory of William Stanford (1764–1841) and another to his son, William Stanford II (1809–59). This second William Stanford left no son but a daughter, Ellen, during whose minority much of the Stanford estate in Brighton and that part of Hove which was then called West Brighton was developed. She married first Vere Fane Benett of Norton Bavant and Pyt House, Wiltshire, who took the additional name of Benett Stanford. Another window in the south wall of the chancel records that Vere Fane and Ellen Benett Stanford restored the chancel of the church in 1878. When he died in 1894 a tablet in his memory was placed on the north wall of the chancel. Ellen Benett Stanford subsequently married Charles Thomas, who took the name of Thomas Stanford and was created a baronet in 1929. He and his wife both died in 1932 and have their own tablet on the north wall of the church. Lady Thomas Stanford had only one son, Colonel John Montague Benett Stanford. His son, Major Vere Benett Stanford, who died in 1922, aged 28 from an illness contracted on active service during the First World War, was the last of the Benetts of North Bavant and of Pyt House and the last of the Stanfords of Preston manor. He has his own tablet in the chancel of Preston church.

During Ellen Stanford's minority and first marriage her mother, Eleanor Montague Stanford, née Morris, continued to live in Preston manor. She married a second time. Her second husband, Captain George Varnham Macdonald, belonged to a Preston family, and both she and her husband are buried in the church-yard, as are their twin daughters, who died as recently as 1947 and 1956 respectively. The daughters also have memorial tablets in the chancel.

In 1531 Preston was united with the then much smaller and less important parish of Hove to the south-west. This union lasted until the death of the Rev. Walter Kelly in 1878. A year later the two parishes were separated by

Order in Council. Walter Kelly, whose incumbency lasted from 1834 to 1878, rebuilt Preston vicarage. In 1908 the church of St John the Evangelist, Preston Road, was built to the design of Sir Arthur Blomfield and became the parish church of Preston.

30

ALL SAINTS CHURCH, PATCHAM

Patcham did not come into the Borough of Brighton until 1928, when the town was expanded to become what was then called Greater Brighton. The pylons, designed by John L. Denman, on the London Road were then erected to mark the northern limit of the new Borough. The village of Patcham lay along the line of what is now the Old London Road and Church Hill. The only building to the west of the main road was Patcham Place, now a Youth Hostel.

The Domesday survey records the existence of a church at Patcham, but this was rebuilt in the twelfth century. The present nave is of this date and the chancel probably also, although most of its features are of fourteenth-century character. The principal feature of the building today is the Norman chancel arch. The 'Doom' painting over it which was discovered in 1883 is probably of early thirteenth-century date. The west tower was added in the thirteenth century, but its broached shingled spire is a nineteenth-century addition. The south porch, though of medieval character, is a post-Reformation addition, probably of the mid-sixteenth century.

Although the church is of medieval construction, its contemporary atmosphere has been largely destroyed by drastic restorations in 1825–30, 1856, 1883 and 1889. On the last of these occasions a very large north aisle was added to the nave which is quite out of proportion to the rest of the building, particularly in height, and has a red-brick arcade that strikes an entirely false note in the interior. This addition was at least built of flints, which are a Sussex material. But at the same time the old portions of the church were refaced with Roman cement. This has killed the exterior stone dead.

The rather florid circular font dates from 1864. The simple but elegant Gothic choir-stalls and reredos probably date from the restoration of 1898.

66 All Saints church, Patcham

On the north wall of the chancel is a memorial to Richard Shelley, who died in 1594.

In the eighteenth and early nineteenth centuries there were three houses in the parish of Patcham whose occupants were important to local history. All three of these families have memorials in the church. The first of these comprised the Paines of Patcham Place. In the chancel are tablets to three generations of John Paine who died in 1768, 1803 and 1874 respectively. The second of these Paines rebuilt Patcham Place in about 1790 and faced it with black mathematical tiles, which were then fashionable. The house is probably the largest single building in Sussex that is faced with this material. This John Paine married Grace Kemp, the aunt of Thomas Read Kemp. She survived him and later married John Hooper.

The second important family was the Roes of Withdean. The first of these was William Roe, who was born in 1748. He was the son of Robert Roe of Brynnwyth in Glamorganshire. After holding office in several public commissions he was in 1788 appointed a commissioner of the Board of Customs and held this position until 1819. For the last fourteen of those years he was chairman of the Commission. He visited Brighton frequently during that period for health reasons or for sea-bathing but always occupied a furnished house. In 1794 he purchased for £13,000 from the Western family, who were landowners in the adjoining parish of Preston, 354 acres of land at Withdean with the manor of Withdean Cayliffe. As far back as 1605 a mansion had been attached to this property. But by the time of William Roe's purchase there was nothing more than a copyhold farmhouse which was sometimes known as Withdean Court or the Old Farmhouse. This was let to William and Thomas Scrase. William Roe never occupied any house on his estate until 1803, when he built a cottage there. In this he occasionally resided for short periods. This may well be either the house on the east side of the modern London Road which is still called Home Farm, or the building on the west side of the road which is now divided into two dwellings known as 'Karibu' and 'Tabora'. Both these buildings date from about 1800. The farmhouse itself no longer exists. William Roe died in 1826, and a memorial to him was erected on the south wall of Patcham church. He kept a short diary from the date of his marriage in 1775 until 1809. This was published by Sir Charles Thomas Stanford in 1928 and gives considerable details of William Roe's Withdean estates.

William Roe was succeeded by his eldest and only surviving son, William Thomas Roe, who was born in 1776. He was a barrister and became junior counsel to the Board of Admiralty. Like his father, he was also a member of the Board of Customs. He died in 1834, aged 57, and also has a memorial on the south wall of Patcham church.

William Thomas Roe's son, Ensign William Dering Adair Roe, perished in a fire in the barracks at Carully in Lower Canada in 1838, aged only 22. His very elegant memorial is in the round-headed recess to the south of the chancel arch. After these two deaths the Withdean estate was inherited by William Thomas Roe's daughter, Eliza Sophia Frances Roe, who married Captain Sir Chaloner Ogle, baronet. She has no memorial in Patcham church, but her husband and son, who both predeceased her, have monuments there. Her husband was the third baronet of that name, his father and grandfather having both been admirals. He died in 1859, aged 57, and is commemorated by a memorial on the north wall of the nave. His son, the fourth baronet, Sir Chaloner Roe Majendie Ogle, died in 1860 aged only

18, and has a tablet in the recess to the north of the chancel arch balancing that to his equally short-lived uncle, Ensign William Dering Adair Roe.

The third important house in the parish was Moulsecombe Place. This now seems so far away from Patcham that it comes as a surprise that it was originally situated in Patcham parish. This house is represented by Benjamin Tillstone, who died in 1829 aged 76. He rebuilt Moulsecombe Place as it is today, which is the headquarters of Brighton's Parks and Gardens Department. His memorial is on the north wall of the north aisle.

One fairly recent vicar of Patcham is perhaps of some interest. This was Canon W. R. Dawson, who was headmaster of Brighton College from 1906 till 1933. On retirement he took the living of Patcham, but was soon forced by ill health to retire, and died in 1936.

31

ST WULFRUN'S CHURCH, OVINGDEAN

Ovingdean came into Brighton in the Greater Brighton expansion of 1928. The atmosphere and character of the few buildings that comprise the original village have been protected from the impact of modern Ovingdean by the belt of trees that surround the grounds of Ovingdean Hall. The church stands to the west of the other buildings, including the old rectory of 1804–7, behind a miniscule green. It is possibly the most attractive medieval church which lies within the Borough of Brighton. It is dedicated to St Wulfrun, who was a seventh-century Archbishop of Sens in France. There is only one other church in England which is dedicated to this saint: the parish church of Grantham in Lincolnshire.

There was a church in Ovingdean at the time of the Domesday survey, but this was rebuilt in the early twelfth century. It comprised the chancel and nave of the present building. The west tower was added later in the same century. At the same time two arches were cut in the south wall of the nave, and a south aisle was built. One arch was similarly cut in the south wall of the chancel and preparations were made for the erection of a south chapel. But this project was not realised for more than 700 years. It is not certain when the south aisle of the nave was demolished. But it is likely that when the French landed on the Sussex coast in 1377 and burned Rottingdean church they may have come on to Ovingdean and have done damage to that building also, as a result of which the aisle was demolished. At any rate this idea was sufficiently accepted to be recorded on a tablet on the south wall of the south chapel when this eventually came to be built in 1907. The whole church is built of flints without stone quoins. The roof was originally of Horsham stone slabs, but most of these have been replaced with tiles. The tower has a pyramidical tiled cap.

67 St Wulfrun's church, Ovingdean

The church was extensively restored in 1865–7, when the south porch was added. Inside, the dominant feature is the Norman chancel arch. This is now flanked by echoing round-headed arches. These were inserted in the restoration of 1865–7. The pews are of the same vintage. The panels of the roof of the chancel were painted at this time by Charles Eamer Kempe, who was born at Ovingdean Hall in 1838. He also designed seven windows in the church: three in the north wall, two in the south wall, one in the south chapel and one in the tower. The last two were amongst the latest of his works as they were executed in 1907, which was the year of his death.

Kempe also designed the rood over the chancel arch, of which the figures were carved in Oberammergau, and the reredos in the chancel, although both these works were carried out later in the century. The reredos was erected in memory of several members of the Anderson family. A scene from the Resurrection to the south of the altar was painted in 1882, the Crucifixion to the north in 1893. The panel immediately above the altar, representing the Entombment of Christ is of painted tiles and rather in the style of Burne-Jones. This dates from 1892. It is partly obscured by a carved wooden screen, which is presumably part of the fourteenth-century rood-screen that was previously attached to the chancel arch. The uppermost figures in the reredos almost at roof level represent St Wilfred and St Richard of Chichester. They were painted at the same time by a local artist named Maude E. Bishop.

There are two later additions to the church. The south chapel was added in 1907 and was the gift of Arthur Carey of Downside, Roedean (since demolished), as a thank-offering for the recovery from an illness. The vestry in the centre of the north wall of the nave was only built in 1984 in memory of Gordon White (1926–82). It was most sympathetically designed by Anthony Whitty. Above the doorway leading into it is a pulpit-like structure on legs which houses the manual of the organ.

The most unusual monument in the church is probably the large board on the north wall of the tower. This was erected in 1832 by Ann Marshall in memory of members of her family who had already been buried at Hurstpierpoint. But after that date and throughout the nineteenth century the early entries were supplemented by later burials which actually took place at Ovingdean. More elegant are the memorials on the south wall of the nave to Nathaniel Kemp and his first wife, Martha. They died in 1843 and 1821 respectively. He was the uncle of Thomas Read Kemp of Kemp Town. Nathaniel built Ovingdean Hall in 1782 and lived there until his death. The house is one of the few surviving buildings in or near Brighton that is faced with buff mathematical tiles. His actual grave is in the church-yard opposite the south door of the church. The tombstone was designed by his son, Charles Eamer Kempe. He was buried in the same grave when he died on 29 August 1907.

Immediately adjoining the south doorway of the church is a venerable yew tree, to which the usual legendary age of 1,000 years is given. It makes the church rather dark. Under it are some interesting table-tombs of red brick and stone dating from the seventeenth and eighteenth centuries. They belong to the Geere family. Also buried in Ovingdean church-yard are the builder, William Willett (1856–1915) who invented daylight saving or summer time, and Magnus Volk (1851–1937) who in 1883 built the electric railway, which is called after him, from the Palace pier to Black Rock.

32

ST MARGARET'S CHURCH, ROTTINGDEAN

Like Ovingdean, Rottingdean was absorbed into the Borough of Brighton in 1928. This expansion was strongly resisted by the then inhabitants of the village who bitterly resented losing their rural status. The High Street has since been very much altered, particularly its south end. But the north end, where this opens out into the Green, still retains some village character. The Green itself is remarkable for the fact that it is still surrounded by no less than nine eighteenth-century or earlier houses of considerable status.

The parish church stands at the north-east corner of the Green. It is very picturesque – so much so that when the cemetery known as 'Whispering Glades' at Forest Lawn, Los Angeles, California, was laid out its proprietors offered to buy Rottingdean church and re-erect it in the United States as the chapel of the cemetery. When they learned that the church was not for sale they did the next best thing available to them by erecting a replica of it instead.

Opinions differ as to the origins of the church. It is likely that a Saxon building consisting of a chancel and a nave existed on the site. P. M. Johnston thought that traces of this church could be seen in the north wall of the nave. Walter Godfrey, on the other hand, thought that no part of the existing building dated from earlier than the early twelfth century. If a Saxon church existed, the Normans began to rebuild this early in the twelfth century as a cruciform structure with a central tower on the site of the Saxon chancel. The present nave is of this date. But it seems that, before the work had been completed, a disaster occurred. The tower collapsed, damaging both the tran-septs and the chancel. The transepts were never rebuilt, although their foundations were discovered during excavations in the church-yard in 1909. The chancel was probably rebuilt in the early thirteenth century. At the same

68 St Margaret's church, Rottingdean

time the nave was widened by the addition of a south aisle of four bays. In 1377 disaster again occurred, when the French landed on the coast and burned the church. After this calamity the south aisle was abandoned and the arcade blocked. At the same time the west wall of the church had to be rebuilt.

From that period onwards no further structural work on the building was undertaken until 1856, when Sir Gilbert Scott restored the church and added a south aisle of three, instead of four, bays and two feet wider than the original aisle. In the process he salvaged one of the fourteenth-century windows and placed this at the west end of the new aisle. He also rebuilt the east wall of the chancel. The west porch was probably added in 1908. Since then only one addition has been made to the church. This comprises the clergy and choir vestries at the north-west corner of the nave. These were very sympathetically designed by Denman & Son and built in 1973–4 by Keith Andrew & Co.

In the eighteenth century box-pews were inserted in the church and in 1818 a gallery was built along the north wall of the nave. This gallery was removed during Scott's restoration of 1856. The box-pews were replaced in 1878. The present west gallery containing the organ and the vestibule behind it were erected in 1908. The original bowl of the thirteenth-century font was dug up in the garden of the vicarage (now called The Grange). This has been placed on the sill of the west window in the south aisle. To provide a new font this bowl was copied and a base reproduced from a contemporary example in Iford church in the Ouse valley.

The most prominent monument in the church is in the north-east corner of the nave behind the pulpit. This is a bust commemorating Dr Thomas Redman Hooker (1762–1838). He was the son of Thomas Hooker of Tonbridge Castle, Kent. He was presented to the living of Rottingdean in 1792 and ministered there until his death in 1838. He built the vicarage to the south of the church, which is now the Rottingdean Branch Library and Toy Museum. Here he ran an academy for young gentlemen, at which the novelist, Edward Bulwer Lytton, afterwards Lord Lytton, was a pupil. The house remained the vicarage until 1908, when it was taken by the artist Sir William Nicholson and renamed The Grange. It was later altered by Sir Edwin Lutyens for the well-known solicitor, Sir George Lewis.

Two other vicars of long-standing have memorials in the church. On the floor of the chancel is a black marble slab in memory of the Rev. Thomas Pelling, who was vicar from 1698 till 1732. The two Burne-Jones windows in the tower commemorate the Rev. Arthur Thomas, who was vicar from 1848–95.

In the eighteenth and early nineteenth centuries one of the principal landowners in the parish of Rottingdean, as in the adjoining parishes of Telscombe, Ovingdean and Falmer was the Beard family of Challoners, who owned a brewery in Lewes. Rottingdean church contains several memorials to members of this family. On the floor of the nave are slabs recording a Richard Beard, who died in 1713, and two Mary Beards, who died in 1726 and 1772 respectively. On the north wall of the nave are tablets to Charles Beard, who lived at the Elms and died in 1870, and Steyning Beard of Down House, who is described as 'the Squire of this parish'. He died in 1909 and was the last member of his family to be prominent in the village.

In the lifetime of Steyning Beard the house at the south-west corner of the Green called The Dene was occupied by Edward Ridsdale. On 12 September 1892 his daughter, Lucy Ridsdale, married in Rottingdean church Stanley Baldwin, who subsequently became Prime Minister. On the occasion of their golden wedding in 1942 Lord and Lady Baldwin, as by then they had become, presented to the church the chair which now stands in the chancel to the north of the altar. Edward Ridsdale is commemorated by a Burne-Jones window in the north wall of the nave.

Two other monuments are of some interest which do not come into any special category. The first is an old memorial on the south wall of the chancel. It commemorates Elizabeth Fothergill of Handsworth in Staffordshire who died in 1800, aged 60, while on a short visit to the sea coast. Her epitaph is one of those delightful catalogues of virtues which make eighteenth-century inscriptions so interesting. 'For though it was often her lot to be like Martha, busied about many things in attending to the interests of this world, yet, like Mary, she forgot not to choose that better part, the looking forward to those of another.' The inscription is too long to quote in full.

The second monument is a fairly recent one on the south wall of the aisle. It commemorates Conrad Arthur Ancrum Betts of the Gonville & Caius College mission camp, Cambridge, who was drowned off Saltdean in 1912, aged 19, and also his companions, Frederick John Taylor, George Henry Allen and Frederick Bedford, of approximately the same age, who also perished when unsuccessfully attempting to rescue him. On the north side of the church-yard is another memorial of death by drowning. This is the grave of David Bennett, Alfred Barnes and two other unidentified members of the crew of HMS *Eurydice*. This ship sank off the Isle of Wight in 1878, and their bodies were washed ashore at Rottingdean. The grave-stone was erected by order of the Admiralty.

It is, however, not the monuments but the stained-glass windows which are the principal feature of Rottingdean church. In 1880 Sir Edward Burne-Jones took two cottages on the west side of the Green and converted them into a single house which he named North End House. He lived there until his death in 1898. Towards the end of this period (1897–1903) his nephew, Rudyard Kipling, resided at the house opposite called the Elms, in the centre of the Green. When Lady Roderick Jones (Enid Bagnold) died fairly recently, North End House was reconverted back into three parts, now named Prospect Cottage, Aubrey House and North End House. Burne-Jones designed five windows in Rottingdean church, which were made in William Morris's factory. The three lancets which were inserted in the east wall of the chancel by Sir Gilbert Scott in his restoration of 1856, were filled with glass in 1893 as the personal gift from Burne-Jones to commemorate the marriage in the church in 1888 of his daughter, Margaret, to Professor J. W. Mackail. The window in the north wall of the chancel was presented by the same daughter herself and represents St Margaret, whose name she shared with the saint to whom the church is dedicated. It bears a Latin inscription composed by her husband. The balancing lancet in the south wall was inserted by the Rev. Arthur Thomas, who was vicar of the church from 1848 to 1895, in memory of his wife, Julia. The two windows in the tower were put up in 1897 in memory of Arthur Thomas himself. Two more windows in Burne-Jones's style are in the north wall of the nave. They commemorate Edward Ridsdale who died in 1901, and Major Roger Rowden, who died in 1918.

Rottingdean church-yard still largely retains its village character. It was enlarged to the north-west in 1883, when the vicar surrendered land on which the disused tithe barn stood. In 1905 the Marquess of Abergavenny, who was the patron of the living and one of the largest landowners in the parish, gave land for a further extension at the north-east corner. This was extended further south in 1920. The sections to the south of this were formerly part of the garden of The Grange (originally the vicarage). These were the gift of Brighton Corporation in 1953 after the house had become a Branch Library and Toy Museum. The southernmost section of all, which is a walled enclosure, was given by Edwin Jukes of Norton House in 1955 and was originally the garden of that house, which is now divided into flats. The land has been left and is maintained as a garden and has not suffered any burials in it. The lych-gate to the west of the church was erected in 1897 as an additional memorial to the Rev. Arthur Thomas.

The ashes of Sir Edward Burne-Jones (1833–98) were buried in the southwest angle of the nave and the south aisle. With him rest his wife, Georgiana (1840–1920), who played an important part in the life of Rottingdean after his death, and their grand-daughter, Angela Thirkell, whose book *Three Houses* (1935) describes the life of the family at North End House during her childhood. Edward and Georgiana Burne-Jones have stone tablets, but Angela Thirkell's memorial is one of those 'bedstead' wooden boards that were very common in the eighteenth century but are now rare because the wood has not survived the passing of so many years. In the modern part of the church-yard is buried G. H. Elliott (the music-hall actor known as 'the Chocolate Coloured Coon').

33

STANMER CHURCH

There was a medieval village at Stanmer, but little is known about it. The Pelham family was connected with the village from at least the sixteenth century, although they seem not to have owned the manor until about 1700. The present mansion (Stanmer Park) was built in 1722–7 by Henry Pelham and his brother, Thomas Pelham. It is the only known complete English work of the architect Nicholas Dubois. Thomas Pelham's son, Thomas Pelham II (1728–1805) was created Earl of Chichester in 1801. The present village to the north-east of the house is an estate village built by the Earls of Chichester in the eighteenth and nineteenth centuries. Besides the church, it comprises a home farmhouse, which was occupied by the bailiff of the estate, a very fine barn, a small almshouse and a number of flint cottages. In 1944 the whole estate was sold by the trustees of the ninth Earl of Chichester to Brighton Corporation and made into a public park. The land on which the village stands was incorporated into the Borough of Brighton in 1954.

The medieval church stood between the village and the mansion. The chief external evidence of its existence is to be found in the two very old yew trees that stand in the church-yard to the north of the present building. Neither Horsfield's *History of Sussex* (1827) nor any other authority gives any description of this church. It was probably a small fourteenth-century building. It was rebuilt in its present form in 1838 by the third Earl of Chichester (1804–86). This is a cruciform building comprising a chancel, north and south transepts, a nave and a west tower, of which the ground floor also serves as a porch. It is built of flints with stone quoins. The tower has an inset broached shingle spire. It is a correct essay in the Early English manner. The architect is not recorded. Nikolaus Pevsner in the Sussex volume of *The Buildings of England* (1965) says: 'If this is not a Victorian remodelling (and

213

69 Stanmer church

there is none recorded) one would like to know the name of the architect.'
Further, the dedication of neither the old nor the present church is recorded.

The principal internal features of 1838 are the west gallery, containing
an organ of the same date, and the painted-glass east window which represents
the Ascension of Christ. The plaster reredos of three trefoil-headed panels
beneath this window is a mid-nineteenth-century addition. The nave roof
of four bays separated by depressed arches supporting six trefoil-headed
panels is a fine piece of work. All the wooden fittings of the church have
special significance as they were all designed and carved by Jude Jones (1844–
1914) who was carpenter and estate foreman to the Earls of Chichester. He
was also a churchwarden and a member of the choir of the church. He must

have had special status on the estate and in the village since his memorial on the north wall of the nave was not only erected by the sixth Earl of Chichester but is the only memorial in the church to be erected after 1838 to anyone but a member of the Pelham family. The front of the pews and the doors of the vestry were designed to match the gallery. In addition to the pew-ends Jude Jones made the altar, the panels containing the Ten Commandments which flank the reredos, the pulpit and the lectern. His son, Francis Jude Jones, generally known as Frank, succeeded to Jude Jones's position at Stanmer. He was bailiff of the farm and organist at the church. He was also a carpenter of talent. As recently as 1965 the double doors of the main west entrance were carved by him and inserted in memory of the seventh Earl of Chichester, who had died in 1922.

A number of monuments survive from the older church on the site. A small brass on the north wall of the chancel records Deborah Goffe, who died in 1626, aged 39. She was the wife of a Puritan rector, the Rev. Stephen Goffe, who is described as 'Preacher of God's word'. Their son, William Goffe, became a colonel in Oliver Cromwell's army and was one of the judges at the trial of Charles I. As a result, he was excepted from the Act of Indemnity in 1660 and had to emigrate to New England.

The most interesting of the old memorials is probably the earliest of the Pelham monuments, on the north wall of the nave. This shows the small kneeling figures of Sir John Pelham, who died in 1580, his widow, who erected the monument, and their son, Oliver Pelham, who died in 1584. The father is described as 'of Pelham's line this Knight was chief and staye'.

The chancel contains three other pre-1838 tombs: a black marble floor-slab, inset with a brass roundel, to Edward Middleton (died 1700); a tablet on the south wall to Elizabeth Scrase (died 1732); and a memorial on the north wall which was erected by the third Earl of Chichester only seven years before the church was rebuilt. This commemorates the Rev. Thomas Baker, who was for twenty-nine years rector of the parish and died in 1831.

The north transept houses the vestry. The south transept has come to be the monumental chapel of the Earls of Chichester. It contains memorials to the third Earl (1804–86), who rebuilt the church, and to the sixth, seventh and eighth Earls. The sixth Earl (1871–1926) died on 14 November 1926, his eldest son, the seventh Earl (1905–26) only eight days later. As a result double death duties had to be paid, which crippled the estate. Less than twenty years later the seventh Earl's younger brother (who had become the eighth

Earl, 1912–44) was killed in a road accident while on active service. This proved a final blow to the family, and three years later the trustees of the ninth or present Earl were forced to sell the whole estate to Brighton Corporation.

Stanmer church-yard has one unusual, possibly unique, feature. Within its bounds stands a well-house. This contains a donkey-wheel for raising water for the mansion. There is another such wheel, but operated horizontally by a horse, behind the house on the north side.

From 1724 to 1727 and from 1771 onwards the livings of Stanmer and Falmer were held by the same incumbent. In 1835 they were formally amalgamated by Act of Parliament. St Lawrence's church, Falmer, was rebuilt in neo-Norman style in 1856. But this is outside the Borough of Brighton and so outside the scope of this book.

34

ST LEONARD'S CHURCH, ALDRINGTON, HOVE

Aldrington originally was a small settlement midway between the village of Hove, which was on the site of Hove Street, and Portslade, now the village of Old Portslade. It was near the then mouth of the river Adur, and its only street probably lay along the line of what is now Boundary Road, Portslade. The population gradually dwindled, and after the great storms of 1703 and 1705 had badly damaged the few cottages that survived, the rate of deterioration grew more rapid. By the beginning of the nineteenth century there were no inhabitants at all. It was not repopulated until the end of the nineteenth century, when New Church Road was extended as far as Boundary Road – Station Street, Portslade. The parish of Aldrington was finally incorporated in the District of Hove in 1893. Five years later Hove became a Borough.

As in the case of Hove, Aldrington parish church stood slightly to the north-east of the village. The medieval building comprised a chancel, nave and small west tower, which were all built in the thirteenth century. By 1586 the church was in a neglected condition. By 1638 it was ruinous. The side walls collapsed early in the nineteenth century. It was rescued from this condition in 1878. Richard Herbert Carpenter was commissioned to rebuild the medieval fabric. R. H. Carpenter designed one masterpiece: Lancing College chapel. Apart from this, his oeuvre was less distinguished than that of his father, R. C. Carpenter. He rebuilt Aldrington church in its original thirteenth-century style with lancet windows. This comprised the south aisle and tower of the existing church. But few if any medieval features survived the process.

Six bells were inserted in the tower, giving the church bell-ringing status. Inside the tower are several boards commemorating special peals. Perhaps the most interesting is a brass plate recording a full muffled peal that was

70 St Leonard's church, Aldrington, Hove

rung on 2 February 1901 in memory of Queen Victoria. From 1879 onwards many burials took place in the church-yard surrounding the church.

During the next sixty years the New Church Road area of Hove filled in with streets running down to the sea. The church, as restored, soon proved not large enough for the congregation. So in 1936 the old building was converted into a south aisle, its north wall demolished and a larger nave and chancel added on the north side. The additions were built of flints in thirteenth century style to match the existing structure. The architect was H. Milburn Pett, who was then architect to the Diocese of Chichester. It was intended to add a north aisle at a later date. An arcade for this was built, and the north wall of the nave, intended to be only temporary, was finished externally in red brick. But this aisle has never been built. A broached shingled spire was also added to the tower in 1936.

The chief features of the new building are perhaps the barrel-vaulted roof to match that of the south aisle and the wide chancel arch. On the south wall of the chancel are a sedilia and piscina in fourteenth-century style. The three lancet windows in the east wall were given by the congregation in 1948. Those in the north wall of the nave date from 1954 and 1961. The organ is a Walker organ and is about a hundred years old. The font in the baptistry at the west end of the nave is a replica of a medieval font with a central column and four surrounding shafts. There are no individual monuments in the church. The lych-gate was built in 1949 to the design of F. A. Crouch.

35

ST PETER'S CHURCH, WEST BLATCHINGTON, HOVE

West Blatchington was originally a downland village. By the nineteenth century it comprised little more than the manor house, which was a large farmhouse, its dependent cottages and ancillary buildings. Its most remarkable feature was one of these ancillary buildings, namely a windmill standing on a barn, erected in about 1820. It is the only secular building of the old village that still stands today. All the remainder have been swept away by the surrounding suburbia. In 1928 the land which made up the parish was divided between the Boroughs of Hove and Brighton, the village portion being incorporated in Hove.

The parish church stood to the west of the manor house, on the west side of the road running north to south which is now Holmes Avenue. The original building dated from the twelfth century and comprised a chancel and nave with some sort of annexe to the west which may never have been completed. Only the nave of this building remains today. In about 1300 the chancel was rebuilt without a chancel arch. By 1596 the building was disused and was regarded as only the chapel of the manor house. By 1700 it was ruinous and by 1830 consisted only of four roofless walls, two of them gabled.

In 1744 the parish was united with the benefice of Brighthelmston, as Brighton was then called. It remained so for nearly 200 years. This added £150 a year to the vicar of Brighton's stipend. During the Rev. H. M. Wagner's incumbency at Brighton from 1824 to 1870 services were held regularly by one of his curates in one of the cottages of the manor house. In 1855 Wagner formed a plan to build a new church in the village at his own expense as a thank-offering for the recovery from a recent illness. He asked the Marquess of Abergavenny, who was the only landowner in the parish, to donate two acres of land for the purpose of building a church, a grave-yard and a school. He even obtained a plan for the church from George Frederick Bodley. When the project proved abortive, Wagner paid Bodley a fee of £10 in compensation for the amount of £30 to which the architect would have been entitled if the church had been built. Lord Abergavenny's tenants at the manor house were then M. H. and G. W. Hobson. They were said to be descendants of the Scrase family, who had been tenants of West Blatchington manor for 400 years. Lord Abergavenny was necessarily obliged to consult these tenants. They unexpectedly refused consent since they were unwilling to give up two acres of their farm-land and did not like the idea of a grave-yard being created there. Moreover they claimed that the eighty inhabitants of the parish at the time, who were of course all their sub-tenants, did not mind the walk of a mile or more to the nearest other place of worship, St Helen's church at Hangleton. The project of building a new church, therefore, did not materialise for another thirty-five years.

On 1 June 1888 Harriet Hobson died, leaving the parish or diocese a legacy to build a new church. Her relationship to the tenants of the manor in 1855 (M. H. and G. W. Hobson) is not certain. A photograph of her which now hangs in the vestry of West Blatchington church shows her in the costume of about 1860 as a middle-aged to elderly woman, so perhaps she was their sister. The consent of the tenant of 1888 must still have been required for the disposal of a smaller piece of land for a church only. Evidently this was available. Perhaps by that time her nephew was in occupation of the manor, unless of course it had passed to Harriet Hobson herself on the death of her brothers.

Instead of building a new church it was decided to restore and reconstruct the ruins of the old building. This was executed in 1890–1. The new church was reopened for worship by the Bishop of Chichester, Dr Richard Durnford, on 29 June 1891. The building comprised the medieval chancel and nave and, in addition, a small weather-boarded bell-turret at the west end of the nave, a small gabled south porch and a vestry at the south-east corner of the chancel. The architect was Somers Clarke, who did so much work in Brighton at that period. The chief medieval feature of the building comprises the two small Norman windows in the west wall of the nave. The trefoil-headed lancet in the south wall, the square-headed window of three similar lights in the west wall and the larger pointed window in the east wall, all in Decorated style, are the work of 1890 rather than of 1400. There

71 St Peter's church, West Blatchington, Hove

is no chancel arch. The roof is barrel-vaulted. At the west end of the nave there is a circular font on an octagonal base. The single sedilia and aumbry in Decorated style in the chancel were replaced and restored in 1940 in memory of the Rev. H. T. H. Wightwick, who was priest in charge of West Blatchington from 1937 to 1939.

No further work was done to the building for seventy years. With the expansion of Hove all round it in the years after the Second World War such a very small building proved inadequate for the needs of the area. The same course was therefore adopted as at Aldrington in 1936, namely to build what was virtually a new church to the north of the old one. The architect was John Leopold Denman. The foundation stone was laid by the Bishop of Chichester, Dr Roger Wilson, on 8 May 1960. It is built of flint and red brick in a style which blends very well with the older building. Unlike Aldrington, the north wall of the old church was wisely not demolished. The two buildings are linked at roof level by an ingenious arrangement of

222

light-wells like a clerestory of dormer windows. Like the old church, the new building has no chancel arch. It is divided into nine bays by coupled ribs of the roof structure which are continued downwards to form arches. At the west end is a gallery containing the organ. This is built over two new vestries. The latter have apsidal ends in the west wall, as does the staircase to the gallery in the south wall. The principal or north front has a series of narrow rectangular windows arranged in threes and flanked by canted flint buttresses.

No pre-nineteenth-century memorials have survived in the church. But when the building was in ruins an ancient brass was salvaged and removed to St Nicolas's church, Portslade, where it can still be seen on the east wall of the south aisle. This records three members of the Scrase family which has already been mentioned: Richard Scrase of Hangleton, who was valet to the Crown and died in 1499, another Richard Scrase and an Edward Scrase, both of West Blatchington, who died in 1519 and 1579 respectively.

On the west wall of the old part of West Blatchington church is a tablet in memory of the Rev. John Hannah (1818–88). He succeeded H. M. Wagner as vicar of Brighton with West Blatchington, but seems not otherwise to have had any special association with West Blatchington church. Curiously enough, he died on the same day as Harriet Hobson, 1 June 1888. Two other tablets nearby record Harriet Hobson's legacy and the rebuilding of the church during the incumbency of John Hannah's son, the Rev. John Julius Hannah (1843–1931).

Burials in the church-yard were made from 1891 onwards. Immediately opposite the south door of the church is the grave of Canon F. Dormer Pearce, who was vicar of Brighton with West Blatchington from 1917 to 1923.

West Blatchington remained united to the benefice of Brighton until the incumbency of Canon G. H. Warde, who held the living from 1939 to 1944. In 1940 the two churches were separated, and West Blatchington was given a parish of its own.

36

ST HELEN'S CHURCH, HANGLETON, HOVE

Hangleton was also a downland village. Like West Blatchington, by the nineteenth century it had dwindled to little more than the church, the manor house, which was about a quarter of a mile to the south-west, and the latter's attendant cottages and farm buildings. The manor house always had a rather grander status than that of West Blatchington. From 1597 until about 1967 it was owned by the Sackville family. The land which formed the parish was incorporated into the Borough of Hove in 1927.

There was a church in existence at Hangleton at the time of the Domesday survey. It stood to the south-west of the village, between it and the manor house. This church was rebuilt from the twelfth century onwards. The surviving medieval building today comprises a chancel, a nave and a west tower. The nave dates from the twelfth century. The tower was added a hundred years later. The chancel was rebuilt in about 1300, but the chancel arch was removed in the fourteenth century. No further additions were made to the church until modern times.

The tide of life began to recede from the village as early as the fourteenth and fifteenth centuries. By the mid-nineteenth century there were only about eighty inhabitants in the whole parish. From 1757 onwards the two livings of Hangleton and Portslade were held by the same incumbent. In 1864 they were formally united as one parish by Order in Council. This union lasted until 1951.

The church never fell into ruins, as did those of Hove, Aldrington and West Blatchington, but only became very dilapidated. Fortunately it attracted private funds and in 1870 was restored at the expense of the Clarenceux Herald, G. F. Cockayne, FSA. Services were held very irregularly, at such infrequent intervals as once a year, but the church-yard was occasionally used

72 St Helen's church, Hangleton, Hove

for burials. The building was again partly restored in 1929. However, as late as that time it was still entirely isolated, and if anyone wanted to inspect the interior they had to go to one of the cottages of the manor house to obtain the key.

The church was rescued from this condition by the extension of Hove to the north-west. This began in about 1936 but did not envelop the whole area until the 1950s. In 1949 the church was more fully restored and reopened for regular worship. The small north porch and adjoining vestry under a joint pentice roof were probably added at this date. Other modern additions were the battlements of the tower and its pyramidical tiled roof or Sussex cap. In 1951 by Order in Council the separate parish of Hangleton was revived.

In the long-run Hangleton church benefited from its under-use in the nineteenth century, for it escaped the heavy hand of the Victorian restorer who often had more money than taste at his disposal. The interior still preserves its medieval simplicity. One special feature of this is the red-brick floor. On the north wall are some wall-paintings which were discovered in the restoration of 1949 and restored in 1969. The earliest of these is the scrollwork within the splay of one of the Norman windows. These are probably of the early thirteenth century. The paintings on the flat wall are of two dates: the fourteenth and fifteenth centuries. The piscina in the south-east angle of the nave is also fourteenth century. As there is no chancel arch the most prominent feature in the church is probably the simple Gothic carved wooden screen. This was erected in 1925 in memory of William Nevett by his widow. He also has a brass memorial on the north wall of the chancel and is buried in the church-yard. The reredos which matches the screen, is of the same date and gift, while the pulpit came from Aldrington church. The only glass of any significance is the east window. This was inserted in 1910 in memory of Sophia Courtney Boyle, who died in 1908. She was the sister of the Rev. Vicars Armstrong Boyle, who was rector of Hangleton with Portslade from 1899 to 1919.

The only monument of any age in the church is in the south-east angle of the chancel. This is a Roman Doric slab like the side of a table-tomb. It represents a husband and wife in Elizabethan costume with their four sons, five daughters and five coffins below to indicate the children who died. The couple have not been identified, but they were probably members of the Scrase or Bellingham families who were tenants of Hangleton Manor for many years. On the north wall of the chancel is a tondo or pieta in memory of Henry Willett (1823–1905) who is also buried in the church-yard. He was a prosperous brewer who at his death left to Brighton Museum a number of valuable pictures and a fine collection of porcelain which is still displayed there as his collection.

The most prominent tombstone in the church-yard is opposite the south door of the church. It is of black marble inset with gold mosaics, almost like cosmati work. It reflects the flamboyance of the person whom it commemorates, Dr Edward Vaughan Kenealy, QC, MP (1819–80). He is, strangely enough, better known for failures than for successes. After unsuccessfully defending Palmer, the Rugeley poisoner, Kenealy acted in the famous Tichborne trial in 1873 as counsel for the unsuccessful claimant, Arthur Orton. This trial created a record of lasting longer than any other trial up to that date. During his defence of the defendant from perjury Kenealy used such intemporate language that he was censured by the jury and as a result was disbarred in 1874. This did not stop him becoming a Member of Parliament for Stoke-on-Trent in the following year. But as no other MP would sponsor him for presentation to the House, Disraeli, as Leader of the House, had to propose a special resolution that Kenealy should be presented without sponsors. He remained a member of the House for only five years and died in 1880. He nevertheless had an extravagant following of his own, and his tombstone in Hangleton church-yard was erected by public subscription.

To the north of the church is the grave of Canon Samuel Augustus Barnett (1844–1913) and his wife, Dame Henrietta Barnett (1851–1936). Canon Barnett, when rector of St Jude's, Whitechapel from 1873 onwards, was well-known for his social work amongst the poor. He founded the Charity Organisation Society (now the Family Welfare Association) and Toynbee Hall, which was the first University Settlement in the East End of London. He was its first warden – a post that has been held by several well-known people since his time. He was also largely instrumental in founding the Whitechapel Art Gallery and the Whitechapel Public Library. Barnett House post-graduate social studies centre in Oxford is named after him. His wife was an equally great social worker. She was the first woman to be nominated as Guardian of the Poor and the founder of the Children's Country Holiday Fund and of the London Pupil Teachers Association. But she is almost certainly best remembered in our time as the founder of Hampstead Garden Suburb, of which the centre was laid out and the buildings designed by Sir Edwin Lutyens.

37

ST NICOLAS'S CHURCH, PORTSLADE, HOVE

The original village of Portslade was what is now called Old Portslade to the north of Southern Cross. Portslade-by-Sea grew up gradually during the second half of the nineteenth century. St Andrew's church, Church Road was built in 1863–4, to the design of Edmund Scott, and enlarged in 1889. It was made into a separate parish in 1898, and at the same date the Urban District of Portslade-by-Sea was formed out of the two parishes. This Urban District was amalgamated with the Borough of Hove in the most recent reorganisation of local government boundaries in 1974.

Old Portslade still retains some village character in High Street and South Street, although this is rather down-at-heel. The parish church and the ruins of the twelfth-century manor house which adjoin it stand on the north side of South Street at its east end where this joins Manor Road. The medieval church comprised the chancel, the nave with its south aisle, possibly the south porch and the west tower. The nave, the south aisle and the lowest portion of the tower were built in the twelfth century. The upper portion of the tower and the chancel were added in the early thirteenth century, except for the battlemented belfry stage of the tower, which did not take form until the end of the fourteenth century. The south porch is of indeterminate age but may pre-date the Reformation. No further addition to the church was made for over 400 years. In 1848 the parishioners petitioned the Diocese of Chichester to the effect that the church was too small to accommodate the whole congregation, and in the following year the north aisle was added to the church. The Brackenbury chapel at the west end of this aisle and the adjoining turret were built in 1869, the vestry to the north of the chancel in 1959.

In the late seventeenth century a gallery for the musicians was built on

73 St Nicolas's church, Portslade, Hove

the south side of the nave. This was removed two centuries later. From 1757 onwards the two livings of Portslade and Hangleton were held by the same incumbent, although they were not formally united by Order in Council until 1864. They were separated again in 1951.

Inside the church the principal medieval features are the chancel arch, the arcade of the south aisle and the thirteenth-century triple sedilia with piscina on the south wall of the chancel. The octagonal shaft of the font in the tower is of fifteenth-century date. The bowl is a nineteenth-century reproduction. In 1847 during repairs some wall-paintings of the Last Judgement were revealed on the south wall of the nave. They were recorded by the vicar of the time, the Rev. Henry Hoper, in a short article in the first volume of the *Sussex Archaeological Collections*, and were dated to about 1440, but were not preserved. Similar paintings were then thought to exist on the north wall also.

The reredos and panelling in the chancel were a memorial of the First World War. They were given by Mrs Blaker in 1921 in memory of her son, Lieutenant Arthur Wilfred Blaker RN, and were designed by F. T. Cawthorn, who had been the partner of Edmund Scott. They were stripped of their varnish in 1934. At the same date the west gallery was erected to the design of the diocesan architect, H. Milburn Pett. It must be one of the highest galleries in existence.

The church contains a good many memorials of interest. The most spectacular of these is the Brackenbury chapel itself. This was erected in 1869 by Hannah Brackenbury to contain the 'mortal remains of the last in lineal descent of the ancient family of Brackenbury of Denton and Sellaby in the County of Durham'. These were her brothers, James Blackledge and Ralph Brackenbury, who died in 1844 and 1864 respectively, the former's daughter, Harriette Mary Brackenbury, who died in 1861, and Hannah Brackenbury herself, who died in 1873. They have separate memorial tablets round the walls, and in the centre of the chapel is a green marble table-tomb giving the escutcheons of the family's descent. Hannah Brackenbury lived at a house in the parish, which was called Sellaby after her ancestral residence. She was a generous benefactor to local charities during her life and by her will.

On the east wall of the south aisle is the ancient brass that has already been mentioned in chapter 35 as having come from West Blatchington church.

The Carpenter, Borrer, Clutton and Blaker families are represented by several memorials each, and the Blakers also have a family vault in the churchyard in the angle of the south aisle and the tower. Perhaps the most interesting are two memorials to members of the Borrer family in the north-east corner of the north aisle. These record two brothers, John and William Arthur Borrer, who both met accidental deaths. John Borrer, aged 29, suffered a coach accident on 17 August 1844 in the city of Carlisle ten days after his marriage. 'Having endured with remarkable fortitude the amputation of his leg, he died after three days of acute suffering. . . . A solemn warning for all to prepare for eternity.' William Arthur Borrer, who was aged 19, 'sailed to Singapore on the 23rd September 1845, and no tidings having been heard of him, it is supposed the vessel foundered in a terrific hurricane which raged in the China seas a few days after he left the port.'

Of the Clutton memorials in the south-east corner of the south aisle, two record the long tenure of eighteenth-century vicars of Portslade. The Rev. Ralph Clutton (1695–1761), who was also rector of Horsted Keynes in Sussex, held the living of Portslade from 1722 until his death in 1761. His son, the Rev. John Clutton (1732–1815), succeeded him and held the living for 54 years. This occupation of the benefice by a father and son for 93 years is not actually a record. In Sullington, also in Sussex, the Palmer family, father and son, held that living for 114 years between them, the father for 45 years and the son for 69 years.

The church-yard of St Nicolas's church, Portslade, is one of the most tranquil and best maintained church-yards in Brighton or Hove. In the south-east portion of it is the grave of William Kerr of the Twelfth Light Dragoons, who fought at the Battle of Waterloo and returned to die in this peaceful spot.

INDEX

(Italicized page numbers
indicate the plate number
of an illustration.)